PADRE MARTÍNEZ
and
BISHOP LAMY

Ray John de Aragon

SUNSTONE PRESS

SANTA FE

Sunstone books may be purchased for educational, business, or sales promotional use.
For information please write: Special Markets Department, Sunstone Press,
P.O. Box 2321, Santa Fe, New Mexico 87504-2321.

Library of Congress Cataloging-in-Publication Data:

De Aragon, Ray John.
    Padre Martínez and Bishop Lamy / by Ray John de Aragon.
        p. cm.
    Includes bibliographical references.
    ISBN: 0-86534-506-6
    1. Martínez, Antonio José, 1793–1867.   2. Catholic Church—Clergy—Biography.
3. Clergy—New Mexico—Biography.   4. Lamy, John Baptist, 1814–1888.   I. Title.

BX4705.M412553D4 2006
282.092'2789—dc
[B]   2006042207

WWW.SUNSTONEPRESS.COM
SUNSTONE PRESS / POST OFFICE BOX 2321 / SANTA FE, NM 87504-2321 /USA
(505) 988-4418 / ORDERS ONLY (800) 243-5644 / FAX (505) 988-1025

CONTENTS

PROLOGUE

Padre Martinez and Bishop Lamy are two of the most colorful and controversial figures in New Mexico history. A much publicized dispute between the two continues to capture the public imagination and has become a focal point of novels, histories and plays. The two men, in their own right, led highly successful careers that peaked with popularity and fame. However, primary interest still centers upon a dramatic rift between them. Many often wonder as to what the actual issues of disagreement were. Of course, there are always two sides to a story. But too often, one finds writers that tend to develop one point of view while sacrificing the other. Such was the case with the Martinez and Lamy conflict. A national best selling novel still continues to place the padre in a bad light while placing Lamy in heroic stature.

Both individuals had their human frailties plus their commendable accomplishments. This book attempts to point out two strong-willed and determined men and the cause and effect that sparked a famous controversy. The first part of this volume deals with the historical setting which sets up the stage for the conflict. The second part is an in-depth study of the issues that touched upon the padre and his bishop, thereby creating the memorable struggle.

As both men were of different backgrounds, ages and cultures, it appears necessary to relate information about their prior history. Reviewing Martinez' and Lamy's past as it deals in relationship to events of the time, one finds the answer as to their cultural conflict. One must remember that New Mexico, at the time, was a newly acquired territory of the United States government. The history of New Mexico was altogether different from that of the United States and Lamy's own native France.

During the year 1848, the United States formally acquired the territory of New Mexico with the signing of the treaty of Guadalupe Hidalgo. New Mexico's history up to that point was one which had shaped the ideas, independent philosophies and personalities of the period, including those of Padre Martinez, which with the takeover would lead to eventual conflicts.

The ancestors of the Hispanic people of the Southwest had lived on the frontier since 1598. Twelve years before the arrival of the pilgrims in the New World, the Spanish colonists had placed their imprint upon the land. New Mexico, Nevada, California, Colorado, Arizona—all bear the names the Spanish first wrote upon their maps, as do countless rivers, mountains, towns and cities throughout the Southwest.

The early Spanish settlers had learned how to survive in the half-desert, half-mountain lands. When English-speaking immigrants arrived in the Southwest they found long established cities, churches and a firmly planted Hispanic culture. The way had been eased for them by the efforts of thousands of colonists that had come before them.

The Southwest was thought of in the East as the Great American Desert. But this began to change when the immigrants saw the lush green fields along the Rio Grande cultivated by Hispanic New Mexicans since the 16th century and the Indians for hundreds of years before that.

The Hispanic New Mexican ranchers, whose heards had roamed the ranges since the early 1700's, introduced the American newcomers to the lariat, branding iron, and the horned saddle. They taught them how to break wild mustangs and round up the longhorns. The Hispanic *vaqueros* (cowboys) taught the Americans the language of the range land and hundreds of Spanish words slipped into the English language. Americans borrowed the words: *arroyo, rodeo, mesquite, bronco, canyon, corral, palomino, pinto, pronto, loco, mesa, fiesta, plaza, fandango*, etc. The word *estampida* was changed to stampede, *chaparejos* was shortened to chaps, *vamos* became vamoose, *juzgado* to hoosegow, and *sabe* became savvy. The famous phrase, "ten gallon hat," came from a Spanish song about a highly decorated *vaquero's* hat, a *sombrero galoneado*.

Five events stand out in New Mexico's history as having touched directly upon every native Spanish surnamed New Mexican with the development of his cultural values: the great Pueblo Rebellion of 1680, the Reconquest by De Vargas in 1692, the popular revolt and civil war of 1837-38, the repulse of the Texas Invasion of 1841, and the United States Occupation of 1846. The events bear heavily upon the conflicting philosophies which were to clash with the arrival in New Mexico of a new church leader, Jean Baptiste Lamy.

The Spanish colonizers had been in New Mexico for eighty-two years when a cloud of discontent began growing and peaked with a powerful Indian revolt in 1680. The Indians felt that the famine and drought which permeated the land were the work of the "devilish" Spaniards that taught them a strange language and religion. Their gods were being wrathful and there was only one way to appease them. Pope spread the seeds of revolt along with other Indian leaders. Some Indians were hard to convince because many of the Spanish had settled far from their pueblos and had gone their own way. Also, the Spanish had protected them from the warlike Apaches and Comanches.

"Yes, but if this is true why do the god's shed their wrath upon us? Was not this land sweet and fruitful before the Spanish came? Did they not cast a spell on many of our people and did they not die of a strange sickness?"

Pope's speech was eloquent. One of the most masterful Indian leaders of all time united a passive people. They became more fierce and vengeful than even Geronimo's Apaches were to become against the Americans two hundreds years later. Bloodshed raged supreme throughout New Mexico and Spain's final venture was apparently over. All of the Spanish were driven out or killed. Attempts at reconquest appeared doomed to failure, until General Don Diego de Vargas petitioned and his venture approved in 1692. The Spanish returned to New Mexico in triumph with Our Lady of the Conquest or *La Conquistadora* as their patroness. Spain was badly in need of a hero and De Vargas filled the need. News of the reconquest reached Spain and he was joyously acclaimed as the last *Conquistador*. New Mexico was again in the colonization process.

The Spanish New Mexicans thanked and praised their patroness for their good fortune. Stories circulated of some having seen visions of *La Conquistadora*. Another story stated that the Indians had made an attempt to storm a Spanish village. But, while the villagers were huddled within their mission church, San Miguel, their patron saint, appeared with drawn sword at the entrance. The Indians fled in panic. Spain's patron, Santiago, according to folklore, continued to appear, leading the New Mexican *Conquistadores* into battle. These were joyous days.

But now it was a time to rebuild even stronger than before. Some of the older settlements were rebuilt and new ones established. Supplies were slow in coming from New Spain and sometimes never arrived. New Mexicans became stronger as the years went by because they were forced to depend upon and defend themselves. Santa Fe, as New Mexico's capital, became a seat of power.

Santa Fe predated the English settlement of Plymouth and was the northernmost seat of government of the Spanish crown in the New World. It far outranked the English settlements in military, political and ecclesiastical activities for decades. Her sphere of influence extended East to the Mississippi, far to the North (near the Arctic regions), to the Pacific of the West and to *La Nueva Vizcaya* (New Biscay) to the South. The governor of this Internal

Province was, for all practical purposes, the ruler of the "Kingdom of New Mexico," and "his decrees carried the weight of royalty."[1]

New Mexico itself, was a medieval enclave in the New World, preserving Old World customs, traditions and language while the rest of Latin America (and the United States) was continually changing through revolutionary development. While all of the events concerned happened before Bishop Lamy arrived in New Mexico, they had set the scene for Padre Martinez' eventual problems with his religious superior.

As an occupied territory, the New Mexicans viewed many of the Americans as intruders. Americans saw New Mexico as a conquered territory, thereby providing the excuse for many to disregard the native cultural heritage, customs and history. Lamy found himself contending with four foreign elements upon his arrival in the United States. As a newly arrived native Frenchman he experienced a cultural shock when he encountered English and German speaking Americans. In New Mexico he had to deal with the Spanish speaking natives. He also had to deal with the heavy concentration of American Indians that were already converted Catholics.

It is not altogether difficult to understand how Lamy must have felt. He was a stranger in a strange land. The only one he felt that he could trust was his boyhood companion, Joseph Projectus Machebeuf. So they both formed what they believed to be, an alliance of survival.

Lamy later tried to create a little France in New Mexico by replacing the native clergy with his own countrymen. He sought to make many changes which were both detrimental and, some consider, beneficial for the land and people. Lamy and Machebeuf were met with distrust. His changes were often met with unacceptance. He experienced a terrific backlash. A backlash most writers have sought to disregard while praising Lamy for his administration and choice of actions. Considering the circumstances, Lamy may not have had any other choice in his ways. But of course his opposition was also correct. One can only form an opinion as to which side was most right. I believe that the unfortunate cultural clash was unavoidable and all concerned were products of a transitional period that marked a new era for New Mexico and her people.

Illustrations

PART I

HISTORICAL SETTING

Stillness filled the air. A fresh blanket of snow covered everything with a serene beauty. An occasional dog's barking could be heard as an echo from a distant time and place. Suddenly the silence was broken and the long wait ended. The church bells of Santo Tomas de Abiquiu sang out their joyous news.

Don Severino Martinez and Dona Maria del Carmel Santistevan were the proud parents of a son.

The date, January 17, 1793, became a memorable one for a peaceful village named Abiquiu[2] and cast a rising glow of enlightenment for a land called New Mexico.

The child was christened Antonio Jose Martinez on January 20, 1793 by the mission priest, Fray Jose de la Prada. After the church ceremony the baptizmal party gathered at the home of Don Severino. They celebrated the occasion with a large meal and prayed for the child. They hoped that he would grow to be a useful and worthy christian in Christ's community. Antonio's father was a landowner, or as they were called then, an *Hacendado*. His lands provided many of the necessities for a fruitful life. New Mexico, during this period, was experiencing peaceful relations with most of the Indian tribes. The settlers raised everything for their provision. What little they obtained from other sources was brought in by way of the long routes to the south, through Durango and Chihuahua.

Don Severino was a kind and understanding man that was well liked and even loved by the people and to many, he was also their *pariente* (relative). The bond of blood made him that much more respected. So the Martinez' joy was shared by all when a son was born to them. Antonio's early childhood was a typical one. From the start he was referred to as a little Don Antonio.

In October of 1797, he entered school at the age of five. One of the servants would take him to and from school. He got into the usual scraps with his schoolmates, but in the end they were all the best of friends.

Antonio's spare time was consistently spent on his studies. He always made sure that his chores were done, for his father would reward his enthusiasm by buying him a book on some business trips to Santa Fe. Young Antonio would carry on debates with his teacher, Don Geronimo Becerra. He would especially feel proud of bringing up a new subject he felt sure the schoolmaster would know nothing about. Every attempt would fail however, because Senor Becerra was a very educated man. Antonio learned his first English from him. He did not realize then that learning English would prove useful in the dim future. Many of the old men of the village marveled at the *sabiduria* (knowledge) of Antonio. Many felt certain he would someday be a great statesman.

By March of 1804, his family moved to Taos which even then was becoming one of the bustling towns in New Mexico. In a short time, it would rival Santa Fe itself in economic and political importance. Antonio made friends easily in his new home town and soon he became well known to young and old alike.

A few months after Antonio's arrival in Taos he witnessed the annual fair. It was held every year in the month of July or August. The people would journey to Taos to sell and trade their goods. The village became an important trading center between the Spanish and the Indians. Their Indian neighbors would take their buffalo hides, pinon nuts, chile and corn to barter at the main plaza. It was always cause for great excitement. Antonio was afraid of the Indian people but he still went out to watch their arrival. He was eager to learn and experience all of the joys and sorrows that the world has in store.

Antonio's parents felt that part of his training for manhood was to become more and more involved with the operation of the *hacienda* (ranch). During the winters, Antonio chopped and carried firewood on his shoulders and in the summers, he tended the cattle. During the spring he learned how to till the soil with a plow. He also helped with the general chores of the home until the age of fourteen when his parents had him work in the fields as he followed the harvest of the crops. He later learned how to manage the country *haciendas*. Don Severino's friends were always more than happy to help him with his son's training. Antonio always proved to be a good, hard worker.

In spite of his many busy days, Antonio always looked forward to relaxing in his room and continuing his studies. He furthered his education by reading, writing and practicing his mathematics. He often recalled Don Becerra's advice,

"If you study every time that you have a spare moment, you will improve yourself and your knowledge will grow as you grow."

Antonio had promised that he would always follow his schoolmaster's counsel.

Antonio was quick to show his horsemanship at the *fiestas* in the *Corrida del Gallo* contest. He had become an expert rider through

3

the years and loved taking care of the horses at the ranch.

Many of the young men of the villages were given the opportunity to display their bravery and horsemanship at the *corrida*. A game-cock was buried in the ground with only its head exposed. The riders, at a distance of a hundred yards, waited for a signal to strike out and snatch the cock while riding by at full speed. [3] Antonio was usually the first to arrive, much to the dislike of his friends. Antonio, often the victor, would ride off with the others hot in pursuit to steal away his prize. At the end his companions would be content with the thought that they'd beat him the next time.

He was always quick to aid his people and even pleaded their cases with his father, Don Severino. The Severino *Hacienda* in time wielded considerable influence throughout the territory. His father's advice was strongly felt in governmental affairs at Santa Fe.

Don Severino finally felt it was time that Antonio should marry being that he was already twenty years old. Antonio objected strenuously but his father's mind was made up. According to the Spanish family's tradition, he had to marry the girl promised to him since birth.

A formal letter was sent by Don Severino to the parents of Maria de la Luz asking for her hand in marriage to his son. After the proposal was approved, the date was set for a *prendorio* (engagement party). Antonio accompanied his parents to the home of Manuel Martinez and his wife, Maria de la Luz Quintana, to formalize the impending event. After being formally received, Don Severino stated, *"Deseamos conocer la prenda que pretendemos"* (We wish to meet the jewel we desire). Maria de la Luz was presented to her future in-laws as Antonio had been. Engagement gifts, usually consisting of gold rings, were exchanged and the engagement became official. The preparations for the wedding now began.

The girl's family spent many days in preparation, sending out invitations to relatives and friends of both families. Maria's mother and *criadas* (servants) worked busily in the sewing room. Don Severino had the food and provisions to be used for the *fiesta* delivered. These would take days to prepare, and out of necessity, made ready for the advance arrival of those that would stay for a few days at the Manuel Martinez *rancho*. Antonio had the *donas* delivered to Maria de la Luz. This was a chest which contained the wedding gown, and several other gowns which Maria could wear at the *fiesta* ball. She would have to go through two or more changes in the course of the evening.

On May 20, 1812, Antonio married Maria de la Luz Martinez.

4

The wedding party left the girl's home in carriages to attend the ceremony to be held in the church. Maria entered the church accompanied by the *padrino* (god-father). Antonio followed along with the *madrina* (matron-of-honor). The parents, relatives, and guests followed in procession and took their places. After the ceremony, the bridal party returned to Maria's home to receive congratulations and have a banquet. The village musicians sang ballads thay they had composed to honor the event at the dinner.⋅ The wedding dance was held in the evening, with Antonio and Maria opening with the traditional *marcha* (march). All of the couples, led by Antonio and Maria, promenaded around the *sala* (hall) and then danced the first waltz. Spanish-Colonial folk dances, which included *Cuadrillas, Inditas, Camilas, Varsovianas*, were played throughout the evening. The festivities ended with the *"Entriega"* (the traditional wedding song) and Antonio and Maria retired to begin their new lives. He had built his home in Taos and expected to earn a living as a ranchman.

Antonio grew to love Maria de la Luz very dearly. Her sweetness, kindness, and loving ways softened his heart. When she was with child they made plans for the future and as with all parents wondered whether it would be a boy or a girl. At the time of delivery a *Partera* (midwife) was called. He sat patiently in their living room for a few minutes and then paced nervously about the room.

He heard a sound and turned towards the bedroom. Yes! The cry of a baby! His heart lightened and a smile crossed his lips. The *partera* entered and a deathly silence filled the room as she said,

"Lo siento mucho pero su esposa ha muerto de parto"
(I'm very sorry, your wife died in childbirth). 5

The moment of joy turned into a nightmare. Congratulations became condolences. Tears streamed from his eyes as he saw his wife's limp and frail body lying on the bed. "Why has God punished me?" he whispered.

At the time of the *velorio* (wake), thoughts kept crossing his mind. "What am I to do now?" Even at the funeral when the last grain of earth was thrown on the grave it failed to seem like reality for him. His wife had died in July of 1813. Their marriage lasting just a little over a year. Antonio sought advice from the priest and his thoughts steadily shifted more to his Creator. He spent much of his time in contemplation and devoted himself to the care of his daughter who had been baptized Maria de la Luz in memory of her mother.

In time Antonio approached his parents with a new thought in mind. He had resolved to serve God by becoming a member of the priesthood. His parents were very pleased with his choice of

5

vocation because they themselves were staunchly religious.

Antonio's eventual adversary, Jean Baptiste Lamy, was born on October 11, 1814 in Lempdes, France. Jean Baptiste was born into a peasant family struggling to carve out an existence in a post-revolutionary France. With his parents, Jean Lamy and Marie Die, he spent his early years in the town of Lempdes situated on a rise near the Alagnon River. His father had once been mayor of Lempdes, one of the poorer towns in France.

Jean Baptiste's parents had a large family, which with time, was met with sorrow. Only four of the eleven children, Louis, Jean Baptiste, Marguerite and Etienne, lived to be adults. There was one consolation for them, three entered into the religious life.

During his childhood, Jean Baptiste began paying devotional visits to the village patroness, Our Lady of Good Tidings at the church. In later years he often prayed there for his family and for his own future well being. He lived in an isolated world. Isolated by geography and the internal unrest his country had experienced. Gazing to the north of Lempdes, Jean Baptiste could pick out two hazy spires of the cathedral of Clermont-Ferrand. It was the only constant and distinguishable feature which could take him out of Lempdes to the city and the world.

Antonio's parents and many of the villagers saw him off late in the winter of 1817. He left his young daughter in the care of his parents. He hugged her and kissed her before leaving. Tears came to his eyes for it would be several years before he would see her again. He traveled on the long lonely road south to Mexico. It was a perilous journey because of the threat of Indian attacks along the way. There were many overnight stops on the trip and, as he heard the coyotes howl in the mountains, he could reflect on events of his past. The death of his wife, the sad eyes of his child Maria, all made him think and hope for the future.

Antonio rode across the arid plain which surrounded Durango, Mexico. It was the location of the seminary and, as New Mexico formally fell under the See of Durango, he would have to study for the priesthood there. The cathedral stood near the center of the main plaza in the colonial city. It was a magnificent structure with a stone facade carved in the Churrigueresque style. The main altar of the cathedral was decorated with gold leaf. Antonio had never seen anything so splendid. In many instances the cathedral rivaled or surpassed those of Europe herself. The bishop's palace was nearby and the seminary several squares away.

Antonio arrived on the 10th day of March, 1817 where he was readily accepted as a student in the Tridentine seminary. Mexico at this time was involved in a struggle for independence from Spain. Antonio, however, devoted himself to his studies and rarely conversed about the political situation. They felt he was just another apathetic New Mexican. New Mexico, in its isolation from the central seat of government, seemed to care little about the independence movement.

He began his studies under Reverend Bernardino Bracho. He quickly advanced in all of his subjects maintaining first place over the other students with the highest grades under all of his instructors. In Scholastic Theology and Moral Theology which he completed at the college, he studied for two years but learned what others learn in three and received a note of superiority. He also received the *Supraloco* for his studies in Arithmetic, Algebra, Geometry and Physics. Antonio eventually began to take turns in acting as the teacher in his respective classes.

During the Lenten season, Antonio had to join the priests along with the other students in the penitential rites. The priests directed secular participation in the act of penance. Things were much more disciplined and self-flagellation, as had been the custom through the ages, was done in an orderly fashion as a group. Antonio was taught that the priest should direct all of the spiritual needs of the people and that he should guide them to salvation.

For Lenten observances, Antonio and his follow students assembled in the church, which was dimly lighted, and a priest moved on to the pulpit. The priest described the torments that await sinners in hell. Upon completion of his discourse, they all joined in prayer. The priest followed by reading passages of scripture describing the sufferings of Christ. At a certain time, the church was darkened with a carved representation of the crucified Christ being the only object illuminated. When a voice was heard saying,

"My brothers! When Christ was fastened to the pillar, He was scourged! " the disciplining began. [6]

Antonio's studies carried him through the war of Mexico's independence from Spain. He had paid for all of his studies until March 9, 1820, when he received a scholarship of royal grace. At the time of the success of the Mexican independence movement in 1821 he was ordained by Bishop Juan Francisco de Castaniza as a minor on the 16th of March 1821. On the following day, he was ordained as a subdeacon, on the 22nd of December of the same year as a deacon, and on February 10, 1822, as a Presbyter.

On February 19, 1822, he gave his first Mass at the college. Antonio was assigned as chaplain of the college. He was to have vigilance over all of his classmates with the title of Underminister. He was also allowed to exercise the ministry in the parish of Durango which was under the charge of Don Bernardino Bracho,

7

until he left on January 23, 1823. He was well on his way to fulfilling his dream of ministering amongst the people.

Lamy, before the age of nine, began his early education with his enrollment at the Jesuit College at Billom. The college was administered by the Jesuit's until the order was suppressed in 1823. The school was then conducted by secular teachers. Jean Lamy proved to be an active student that strived to perfect himself in all of his studies.

The Spanish flag was lowered and the Mexican flag raised at the Palace of the Governors at Santa Fe without much fanfare. A proclamation was read and some of the officials called for the residents to attend. News of the independence spread slowly through New Mexico's isolated mountain villages and in some cases never reached them.

Padre Martinez left the college lacking only one year of completing his optional course in Scholastic Theology in January of 1823. He had already complied with his required study in Scholastic Theology with high honors. He left because he fell ill of a palpitation that impaired his breathing. After recovering in the home of his parents, he reported and asked for more time while he occupied himself in the ministry. His superiors granted what he asked for.

On returning to New Mexico Padre Martinez found her religious state in a deplorable condition. Most of the Franciscan priests had been recalled after independence and the few that remained did so because of old age or illness. He became anxious to get out and do more for the people. Padre Martinez lent himself with good faith and charitable promptness as the urgency of the situation required. Reverend Father Fray Sebastian de Alvarez, who was in office the year of his arrival, was very pleased with his sound religious and political conduct.

On November 24, 1823, with approval from the Honorable Governor of the Sacred Mitre, Antonio was placed as substitute curate for Father Francisco Ignacio de Madariaga. Father Madariaga was a secular priest of the Immaculate Conception Church at Tome, New Mexico. He and his parents rejoiced at his new appointment. On his journey to Tome, young Padre Martinez prayed for his success as a Servant of God, bringing all of the people to the fold of Christ. When he arrived in Tome he was given a warm reception by the people.

The people of Tome quickly learned to love and respect Padre Martinez because of his dedication to the religious life. They began to speak everywhere of the padre's eloquent sermons. His sermons even brought those that felt it a burden rather than a privilege, to attend Mass. The padre's inner peace, and outward

frankness and kindness drew the people to him. Members of lay confraternities that were dedicated to Mary or the saints began volunteering their services. He had pleased everyone with his sermons and had gained many friends until the termination of his stay on March 10, 1824. He had only been a substitute for the mission priest but he had proven that he would be a good minister to the people.

In July, 1824, Padre Martinez asked the territorial assembly to secularize the Taos Mission because of the lack of priests in New Mexico. The assembly made a report, August, 1824, to the Bishop of Durango asking that the missions at Taos, Abiquiu, Belen, San Miguel del Bado and San Juan be secularized. The secularization of the mission churches would not begin until 1826. The assembly at that time, brought it to the attention of Vicar General Augustin de San Vicente on his visit to New Mexico.

The year 1825, promised to be a good one according to all indications. Although the work was slow and tedious, Padre Martinez felt that in time he would attain his goal. His daughter provided a much needed comfort on especially trying days. When she suddenly became ill Antonio continuously prayed for her recovery. At times she seemed to get better, but in the end the Lord took her in November 1825. It was almost too much for him to take. People from all over the territory offered their condolences. Again he spent hours in contemplation and prayer. He found an inner happiness in the thought that both his wife and daughter were in the presence of the Lord and although the hurt was deep, he would continue to answer the call to serve Him.

Padre Martinez' life became a dedication to the service of his people. Everywhere he traveled the people readily accepted him. It was more to them than a mere sharing of his misfortune. The padre's commanding appearance and his personal magnetism served as an inspiration.

Padre Martinez was persuaded to enter governmental affairs by his family. He saw in this another opportunity to aid the people. The Mexican government commissioned him as the consulman for the Americans entering into New Mexico because of his knowledge of the English language. The padre's duties were to protect the interests of the Americans as well as seeing to it that they respected the laws of the land. The official document which he received began with the following words:

"Instructions to be followed by Father Don Antonio Jose Martinez to perform the duties of his position, for which he is herewith authorized adequately by this government on said date," it ends with: "Leaving in safety the frankness by which this affair should proceed by the commission, many times I

10

implore that your operations should be deliberate to extremes so that nothing will result in complications. Santa Fe, April 1, 1826, ANTONIO NARBONA."

Narbona was then the governor of New Mexico.

On May 26, 1826, the young priest was given the administration of Santo Tomas de Abiquiu by Vicar General Don Agustin Fernandez de San Vicente. The church of his native home was an *asistencia* (dependency of the parish church) of Santa Cruz de la Canada. The mission church of Abiquiu had earlier been under Fray Teodoro Alcina de la Borda. He gave jurisdiction of the church to the last member of his order to be there, Fray Sanchez de Vergara. A secular priest, Cura Leyva y Rosas, took over in 1823 before Martinez was assigned to take his place in 1826.

Abiquiu, along with Tome and Taos became officially secularized on May 26, 1826. Padre Martinez because of the extra studies that he completed, received on January 18, 1826 more extensive powers. They were given on recommendation of the Ecclesiastical Council. He was addressed in the following words from Secretary of the Council, Prebendary Don Juan Bautista de Olmo:

"Because of the great praise and fame that is your desert, the venerable council instructs me to assert..." The priest was given authority to, "celebrate two masses on feast days, *absolve from reserved sins,* to make and revalidate marriages *intra confesionem*, to give blessings in which the unction of the Holy Oil is not used and to give plenary indulgence to the dying, *all for as long as he chooses.*"

On July 23, 1826, Martinez was given the curatorship of Taos by the Vicar General and he soon saw himself spread thin. Padre Martinez received a visit from San Vicente. Padre Martinez in conversing with the vicar found an opportunity to recommend the establishment of schools in Pueblo, San Fernando, and San Francisco de las Trampas. *Nuestro Padre San Francisco en el puesto de las Trampas* was on present day Ranchos de Taos, three leagues (about nine miles) from Taos Pueblo. It should not be confused with the church of San Jose de las Trampas which is south of Picuris. The chapel in Ranchos de Taos was not completed until 1815 when the provincial custos was Fray Isidoro Barcenilla. The chapel was later placed as a visita to San Geronimo where Fray Pereyro was later assigned. [7] The vicar questioned the priest about his work at the chapels of Santa Rosa de Lima and Santa Cruz del Ojo Caliente.

San Vicente in his inventory of Ojo Caliente, a visita of Abiquiu, described a retablo painted in tempera with seven images: St. Anthony and St. Francis, the Holy Trinity, St. John Nepomuk, Our

11

Lady of Guadalupe, St. Raphael and "the Holy Cross which is the founder." It was noted that the people of Ojo Caliente were so poor that they did nothing to provide for the church, which was poorly furnished with "pulpit, confessional, an old metal censer, ten wooden candlesticks, one wooden chair and a baptismal font of copper." These were mostly supplied by Padre Martinez.[8] The padre on occasion, also said Mass at the church of Santa Cruz de la Canada.

After examining his records and finding them satisfactory he told the priest that his recommendations would oe taken under consideration and forwarded to the See of Durango. It was also noted that the young padre was,

"conducting himself with the faithful of the parish and with the authorities with the greatest harmony, affection and upright political conduct, succoring the needy with alms, and very particular not to burden the poor with fees whenever he found it possible to spare them."

He was also serving as delegate minister of the Third Penitential Order of St. Francis placed in charge of the devout of the parish of Taos by the Father Custodian. Padre Martinez, however, felt the need to resign his position in Abiquiu on September 1826 to devote himself fully to Taos.

In May of 1827, Padre Martinez was petitioned by thirty families from Rio Chiquito. Bernardo Duran, their representative asked for permission to celebrate the Mass of Our Lady of St. John as their patroness. The authorization given by Martinez reads:

"In this Pueblo of San Geronimo de Taos today, the eighth of May, 1827, Don Bernardo Duran appeared before me, a citizen of Rio Chiquito, a part of the quarter of San Francisco de las Trampas, within the actual limits of the said quarter, requesting that he be given a document in writing for which I give him this one. Because the residents of this plaza of Rio Chiquito and its adjacent ranches hold as their special Patroness the Virgin Mary in the title of the Lady of San Juan. They have promised to celebrate her feast in the church once every year and, to begin, will hold it on the first of December and on those of the following years.

"For the Mass (they will pay) one pound of beeswax, for the privileges of the sung Mass with a procession, six fanegas of corn and wheat, between the one and the other. If there are vespers, two fanegas of grain.

"Those included in the said devotion to Our Lady of St. John are a little more than thirty heads of families with those others who add themselves, and by this act become separated from the function that is celebrated by the devotees of St.

Francis, but only in the summertime. They wish to continue with that somewhat, and shall be included in helping to support the chapel of St. Francis at el Rancho. For the due faithful and comfort of their solicitude, to the said residents of Rio Chiquito it is agreed. It is understood that the citizen, Senor Rafael Tafoya, is named mayordomo for the function to be held this year since it was settled before. I give said document to the said Don Bernardo Duran today, as of this date, the which I sign with my pen and hand. ANTONIO JOSE MARTINEZ." [9]

During the month of June of 1827, Martinez' father became ill and died. Don Severino left extensive lands which were scattered around Abiquiu, El Rito and Taos. Many of the tracts of land already had houses on them. Don Severino also left a large quantity of live stock, textiles, silver of eight hundred *pesos* plus more than eight hundred *pesos* owed to him by others. He also owned a thirteen piece dinner set made of silver.

As the eldest of the children, Antonio had to assume the transfer of his father's estate as an executor along with the help of his brother-in-law, Manuel Martinez. Much of the estate was passed on to Don Severino's wife, six children, and two servants. A large number of livestock and some money was distributed to the poor. Padre Martinez became very sorrowful not only because of his father's death, but also because he had to neglect his people to some extent. They however, accepted it as the faithful duty of a loving son to his father in fulfilling his wishes. Antonio spent from June 30, 1827 through February 20, 1829 executing the provisions of his father's will plus complying with the duties of his ministry.

On Commission of the Vicar Don Juan Rafael Rascon, Martinez was put in charge of the mission of San Lorenzo de Picuris in March of 1829. At the same time, Padre Martinez turned his attention to a problem which had long bothered him, the church's tithing.

When the friars first came, the tithes were not entirely intended for themselves. Each mission church had its own field for which the missionaries had to provide seeds and, when the Indians were unwilling even the labor. Tithes in the form of food were stored in the convents after harvest for use of the clergy as well as the Indians. In case of crop failure or enemy raids, the missionaries provided food from their stored supplies.

The clergy had maintained a policy of the payment of tithes for the administration of ecclesiastical services. The settlers willingly gave a chicken for a Baptism or two eggs for a Mass in order to help the missionaries survival in the harsh land of New Mexico. However, as time passed by, the growth of the church began to require a steady increase of tithes for its upkeep. Apparently, by Padre Martinez' time, the collection of tithes was out of control. Tithing had gone from a voluntary basis to a mandatory one. All those unable to pay the fees set for ecclesiastical services were forced to go without having their children baptized, their dead had to be buried away from the sacred ground of the church, or go without a church wedding if they could not pay for that particular service.

Numbers of unmarried couples living together began to rise and others began to steal in order to pay the tithes so as not to go without the sacraments of the church. Of course, many were caught and jailed and their cases became a pathetic sight in the courts. [10] Padre Martinez rose to the crying need of his people and traveled to the courts to state their cases. He also made several donations to the church. The priest distributed some seeds each year in the different settlements among the needy. He always gave seeds or articles of clothing to those who asked for them at his home. He spent sleepless nights seeking an answer to the cessation of such tithing.

He wrote a treatise in which he denounced such practices as detrimental to an individual's well being as a citizen as well as a Christian. Armed with his discourse he set out for the Territorial Assembly in Santa Fe where he stated his case. His reasoning so moved its members that they sponsored a trip for him to the National Congress in Mexico City. His exposition was published in all of the newspapers of the Republic. He soon enjoyed the support of an overwhelming majority.

Political leaders in New Mexico strongly supported his enthusiastic struggle and he was appointed in 1830 to the Departmental Assembly as Territorial Deputy. In this position he found an avenue to espouse his cause. Padre Martinez remained in the position until 1831.

During the month of August of 1830, Vicar Don Juan Rafael Rascon visited Padre Martinez at the parish and chapel of Taos. The entries in all of his books were approved and all of his marriage records, sentences copied.

In the same year the padre was prevented from making the trip to Durango to attend the Concursus. He could not find a priest to leave in charge of Taos and Picuris. He had been giving two masses on feast days in two churches. At times preaching in both, although always in one of them. The priest would sometimes say Mass in the church of Abiquiu or Picuris and then in the church of Our Lady of Guadalupe at Taos. The distance between the churches was as much as seven leagues (almost twenty one miles). He would also serve in other areas at the same time. But Martinez was told that this was no discredit to him.

"He could not be given an official appointment as pastor by virture of competition as he had not gone,"

replied the secretary of the Ecclesiastical Council.

In April of 1831, some of the brothers from Santa Cruz appealed to hold their Lenten exercises in Taos. On April 6th, their request was forwarded to the Vicar and Visitor General, Don Juan Rafael Rascon, in Santa Fe, for approval. On April 12th the vicar issued his approval but with a stipulation that they should exercise due moderation in their penitential observance during Holy Week. [11] After the end of the Lenten season Padre Martinez continued his fight against tithing. He also resigned his position at Picuris because of his extensive duties. His resignation was duly accepted and his reasons noted.

Jean Baptiste Lamy, after nine years at the Jesuit college, had determined to make the priesthood his life's vocation. He entered the preparatory seminary of Clermont at the age of eighteen in 1831. Upon completing his studies in Clermont he was admitted to the diocesan seminary of Mont-Ferrand for the course of theology in 1832. Mont-Ferrand, which was situated on the outskirts of the city, was administered by the Sulpicians. There Lamy met his lifelong friend, Joseph Projectus Machebeuf. Machebeuf was two years ahead of Lamy and thereby was the leader in the friendship and often helped the younger seminarian.

Bishop Benedict Joseph Flaget returned to his native Auvergne from the United States in 1833. In talking about his experiences in America, Flaget inspired others, including Lamy and Machebeuf, to minister there. But they were still seminarians, and it would take Lamy six years to complete his studies in theology before they could go out to see the new land.

Others in the Mexican Republic began to take up Martinez' crusade by writing similar discourses against church tithing. The matter reached a climax in 1833 when it was deliberated upon in a special session of the Federal Congress. After a four year struggle on the part of the priest, *the tithing was removed.*

Padre Martinez felt certain that his bishop, Don Jose Antonio Laureano de Zubiria, would call upon him to answer for his conduct. Many feared that the good priest would be censured. But word arrived from the tolerant bishop which was quite to the contrary. In the bishop's official statement he pointed out that he considered the priest's fight as,

"The opinion of a priest in the capacity of a citizen, recognizing the right he had, under the Mexican Constitution, to express his opinions in political matters."

On July 6, 1833, Bishop Zubiria made an episcopal visitation to

New Mexico and examined Padre Martinez' records at the Our Lady of Guadalupe Church at Taos, the church at Ranchos de Taos, the church at the pueblo, San Geronimo de Taos, and its visita, San Francisco de las Trampas. The entries in all of his books were approved. The fulfillment of his ministry compared favorably with that of his predecessors. In the certifying entries made in the parish books by the bishop was acknowledged that he was given thanks and urged to continue in the same tenor.

While in New Mexico, Zubiria let it be known that Pope Gregory XVI had given him faculties to delegate priests to administer the Sacrament of Confirmation. Such authority had always been reserved to bishops. Padre Martinez as pastor of Taos and Padre Madariaga as pastor of Tome were the two selected by him to receive the honor. Padre Martinez however, was granted more extensive authority, rights, and duties in his administration in northern New Mexico.[12] At this time after convocatory edict for competitive examinations, he withstood the synod with the object of being officially appointed permanent pastor. Zubiria could not

16

make the provision because of the critical circumstances of the political state in that year. A certain supreme decree prevented in a general way such a step. Although circumstances improved later, no official appointments were made.

The priest mentioned to Zubiria that he had been given a delegation as minister to the Third Order by his predecessor and showed him the offical document. The bishop found everything in order and gave his approval to the delegation. Martinez mentioned to Zubiria that many of the young boys had approached him with the thought of dedicating their lives to Christ by entering the priesthood. Bishop Zubiria took note and felt that their education was too limited for them to succeed with the rigorous studies in Durango. Padre Martinez appealed for the bishop's permission to establish a school at Taos. He could instruct the students at his own expense, in preparation for the priesthood. Zubiria gave his approval and commended the padre's work and efforts on behalf of the people of New Mexico. They had a pleasant meeting which ended with the bishop telling him to "keep up the good work."

The bishop then continued his visitation on up to Santa Cruz where he became astonished when he discovered that there existed a flagellant group of Penitentes there. Upon questioning their priest, Don Jose Francisco Leyva y Rosas, about them, Zubiria was told that the Penitentes were members of the Brotherhood of *Nuestro Padre Jesus Nazareno*. They also referred to themselves as brethren of the Third Order of St. Francis.

The bishop became angered at the thought that a society had existed without his approval or without the apparent knowledge of his predecessors at Durango. However, the Vicar General Rascon and more than likely Fernandez de San Vicente [13] most certainly knew about them but overlooked the group since they had priestly guidance. Rascon himself had begged that they not commit excesses in their penitential rites. They had also recognized the Brothers as active members of what was thought to be a very much alive Third Penitential Order Brotherhood of St. Francis. Thus, they could have failed to report this to the bishop at Durango.

With Zubiria's approval, Padre Martinez opened the seminary of *Nuestra Senora de Guadalupe* on July 15, 1833. He started out with four students, two of which were orphans. All started from the beginning of Grammar, or the declensions of the nouns. Padre Martinez went as far as setting up a dormitory type of residence for those youngsters that lived too far to attend classes on a regular basis.

On his return to Santa Fe, Zubiria denounced the associations in a decree dated July 21, 1833. He directed it to all the parishes in New Mexico and especially to those in which chapters of the

17

Brotherhood might exist. Zubiria felt that he could not condone such an association of men that practiced public self-flagellation and even crucifixion. Part of the decree reads as follows.:

"There is, beyond a doubt, a Brotherhood of Penitentes at Santa Cruz de la Canada which had already been in existence for a number of years, without authorization or knowledge of the bishops, who certainly would not have given their consent to such a Brotherhood, even if it had been asked. The very open, excessive corporal penances which they are accustomed to practice on certain days of the year, even publicly, are quite contrary to the spirit of Religion and the regulations of the Holy Church. Among other things or inproprieties which it is possible to bring up, there is nothing which conforms to Christian humility.

"In order that such practices not be allowed to remain unmanageable, even the construction of a room intended for the housing of instruments of mortification or meeting of Penitentes, if they should ask, may not be permitted by any Priest. If *they sometimes flagellate themselves with due*

moderation, they have a place of worship in which they can congregate. Since it is necessary to put an end to the abuses of this kind, which will sometime bring grief to the Holy Church, trusting the conscience of our parochial priests in this villa, both present and future, we strictly command that in the future they not permit such meetings of Penitentes for any reason. The room in which they have kept their crosses, etc., if not the property of a definite individual, may remain in the service of the Holy Parochial Church. The aforesaid instruments must be destroyed, although each one may take his own to his house, without its ever again being used by a congregation or Brothers of such a Brotherhood of Penance, which we annul and which must remain no longer active. All are ordered to strict obedience in this rule of the Prelate, penance being one of the most acceptable sacrifices which can be made in the eyes of God.

"And we furthermore decree with equal strictness that if the priest of this parish comes to understand that there are any other such meetings of Brotherhoods of Penitentes in parishes of this territory, in order to prevent them, he must advise the appropriate priest, mentioning this Decree, for we do not wish other similar abuse in any area of this Territory...

"Moderate penance, which is beneficial to the spirit, is not prohibited; but totally illegal gatherings incorrectly called Brotherhoods are. Each one who is of good faith and desires self-penance, not destruction, must take up the usual instruments, but they must take them up in private."

Bishop Zubiria, however, did grant a concession in that he would allow self-mortification privately in moderation but not publicly in associations.

Padre Martinez took the news to the Brothers, and also stated that it was inevitable that the Brotherhood would have to disband if they continued public displays of self-flagellation. But, they could continue with the bishop's approval as Tertiaries of St. Francis. The Penitentes appealed to their Conciliador and begged for his help as their Superior [14] so that their faithful Brotherhood would not come to an abrupt end.

Padre Martinez turned his attention towards the condemnation and wrote the stirring, *"Defense of the Holy Brotherhood."* [15] Tradition has it he specifically defended the Brotherhood of *Nuestro Padre Jesus Nazareno,* giving its history, statutes and pious objectives.

In November of 1833, Zubiria assigned the mission of San Lorenzo de Picuris to Padre Martinez. Also in the same month and year the priest received three more students to study for the

19

priesthood. By November 1834, he received another three students at his seminary at Taos. His first students had already finished studying grammar or the declensions of the nouns and had learned Latin Grammar and Moral Theology. The padre advanced a sum of money to Juan de Jesus Trujillo and Eulogio Valdez for their journey to Durango to take the Orders. Mariano Lucero, another student, paid his own way.

Several years after the Mexican independence many officials had felt that the central government was not exercising enough jurisdiction over her territory. Therefore, in 1834 a new constitution was adopted by the Mexican National Congress, under which the national territory was to be divided into departments. Governors were to be appointed, and an election of departmental council members held. In essence, the division of the territory into departments would have some similarity to the organizational set up of states in that the congress could exercise greater jurisdictional authority over the national territory.

By 1835, due to the scarcity of textbooks and instructional materials, Martinez sought and obtained a printing press. He was able to solicit the aid of an experienced printer by the name of Jesus Maria Baca, who in turn taught the priest's students the art of printing. The padre spent every spare moment in the writing and development of materials. He wrote and printed spelling, grammar, arithmetic, social studies and theology books. During the early years of his school he touched upon language arts in Spanish, Latin and later in English. Padre Martinez' students helped him run the printing press on which he began to publish volumes directed at the general public. Volumes on law, government, and theological treatises steadily appeared.

The Mexican government sent Governor Albino Perez to New Mexico in April of 1835 to assume the duties of *Jefe Politico* (Political Chief) and commanding military officer. His chief duty was to impose the new form of government called for by the newly adopted Mexican constitution. To New Mexico it meant direct intervention by Mexico in the province's ability to determine her own future and state of affairs. Albino Perez was not very popular in New Mexico although he did try to improve educational and economic conditions.

Early in the year of 1836, two of Padre Martinez' students, Trujillo (later assigned to the parish of the villa de Santa Cruz de la Canada) and Valdez (later assigned to the parish of Santo Tomas de Abiquiu), were ordained in Durango by Zubiria. Lucero was ordained in October of 1836. In 1837, he would help Padre Martinez in the administration of the parish of Taos and Picuris. Five other young seminarians left for Durango to be ordained.

Padre Martinez later began to receive help at his seminary with other priests that started to teach there. His school began to grow and gain in popularity. Several priests were eventually assigned to aid Martinez as his coadjutors or assistants in his extensive ministry in northern New Mexico.

The departmental assembly, within a year of the arrival of Perez, passed a revenue law. The law which was approved by the City Council and signed by Governor Perez on the 9th day of June, 1836, was primarily enforced on New Mexicans. All of the entries into Santa Fe were blocked off by the Perez militia. A tax of two dollars was charged for each vehicle entering the city of Santa Fe with foreign merchandise. Anyone driving herds of cattle or sheep through the streets of the capital would have to pay from twenty to twenty-five cents per head before selling the animals. Santa Fe was the only large livestock trade center at this time. Therefore, the Hispanic New Mexican *rancheros* were forced to drive their herds to the capital. The only other alternative was to take them on a long journey to Chihuahua.

The ranchers associations began to hold meeting against the taxation. Perez, realizing that the ranchers could not find *vaqueros* (cowboys) for a drive to Chihuahua, would not repeal the tax.

New Mexico was a frontier land where life was hard and the sacrifice demanding. However, the pioneer New Mexicans sought every means of entertainment to make life a little easier and less painful. They held *fandangos* (dances), once a month, to socialize with their *amigos* (friends). The *fandango* ball provided a much needed relaxation and the problems and politics of the day could be discussed openly and heartily. The young ladies and gentlemen of the *villas* would look forward to the ball and many spent hours practicing the stately waltzes in their free time. The melodious waltzes served as a link with seventeenth century Europe. French, Austrian and Spanish waltzes, once the rage of the European courts, were still wonderfully preserved in early 19th century New Mexico.

The Hispanic New Mexicans held *mystery plays* (religious dramatizations) during the Holy Season of Christmas to commemorate the birth of Christ. This was another means of providing entertainment in the seasons when *fandangos* could not be held. The social events were usually held in the home of a *ranchero*. The *hacienda* selected often had an unusually large sala to accommodate everyone. The New Mexicans were shocked to learn that the new bill of taxation called for the payment of $2.00 for theaters (theatrical entertainment) and all other entertainments. The license for *fandangos* was set at fifty cents for each dance. Money was very scarce in New Mexico, but the militia was

21

quick to jail anyone attempting to barter for the payment.

All foreigners as well as Hispanic New Mexicans residing outside of Santa Fe had to report themselves to the *Alcalde* within three days after their arrival in the capital. Each one had to state his business and occupation and on failure to do so, were fined $10.00 for each violation of the law.

The new government began to grant large donations of property (land grants) to wealthy Mexicans. Thus leaving the masses or the poor population without a way to earn a living. Padre Martinez wrote,

"This practice is based on an injustice observed by a government whose tendencies are not in agreement with the advancement of the people." [16]

The taxation of his people again became a concern for Padre Martinez. This time it came from the government rather than from the church, and to some extent with more drastic results. It stymied the productivity of the land. Life became unbearable to many. The threat of harsher impositions brought the matter to a head with the priest's publication of a newspaper titled *El Crespusculo de la Libertad* (The Dawn of Liberty). [17] He attacked the taxation as a demeaning and unbearable burden upon a people already tormented by drought and constant attacks by Indians. Padre Martinez took up the defense of his people as he had done against the church's tithing. He again hoped to force the removal of this new taxation with appeals and persuasion. But the resentment of the people turned into a full fledged and uncontrolled revolt in an attempt to win back their dignity. *El Conciliador* repeatedly called for a peaceful change by which the same purpose could be achieved through diplomacy. They answered him that it was time for action, being that force was the only thing that the oppressor understood. The priest's fight then became a relentless struggle to avoid the shedding of peoples' blood.

Life in New Mexico was barely livable without being subjected to such, as was thought, "unjust measures." The padre was elected to the Departmental *Junta* on April 30, 1837. He served as a judicial officer, since he had studied canon law, the civil laws of Spain, and the laws of Mexico. He recommended names of a native replacement for Perez to the Assembly.

The Padre became more alarmed with the cry of war that rang in the air. He called a meeting with the leaders of the planned rebellion. They came and listened to their priest but his efforts at maintaining the peace were to no avail. Their minds were made up. They had won over the support of the Pueblo Indians. There would be no stopping them now. Their cause, they felt, was a

22

sacred one and for the benefit of all New Mexicans. At his church of Our Lady of Guadalupe the Padre begged for the cessation of hostilities in his sermons. Padre Martinez counselled that their vengefulness was not in keeping with God's commandment of, "Thou shalt not kill." But the people did not listen to their priest. They told him, they realized that as a man of God, it was his duty to seek peace. The revolutionaries stated, it was their obligation to take up the sword of their forefathers and strike down this intrusion upon their soil.

The people's revolt began with the cry of

"Long live Our Lady of the Conquest. Down with oppression; down with bad government."

A liberation army was organized with the primary objective of laying seige to Santa Fe. It would take over the control of the capital and set up a new government. On the 3rd of August of 1837, the leaders of the revolution developed a platform which declared,

"Long live God and the nation and the faith of Jesus Christ for the principal points we defend are the following:

1st.   To be with God and the nation and the faith of Jesus Christ.

2nd.   To defend our country to the shedding of our last drop of blood to obtain the victory sought after.

3rd.   Not to admit any plan of department.

4th.   Not to admit any taxation.

5th.   Not to admit the bad orders of those who are trying to effect it."

News of the massing of an army at Santa Cruz de la Canada reached Governor Perez. He appealed for aid from Mexico but to no avail. He finally determined to go out and encounter the rebel forces near the mesa of Santa Cruz. His army was thoroughly routed. Indications from advanced intelligence had failed to verify the exact number of enemy forces. Perez, with less than 200 troops, was surrounded by more than 2,000. He, with a few others, had been watching the battle and escaped to Santa Fe. They gathered their belongings with the anticipation of fleeing the territory of New Mexico.

Perez and his men were, however, captured and killed by Indians that were aiding the revolutionaries. The New Mexican liberation army, after the battle of Santa Cruz, advanced to Santa Fe where they set up a provisional government. On August 10, 1837, they paid homage to *La Conquistadora*, in the church for their victory.

An election was held by the members of the army. They selected Don Jose Gonzales as provisional governor and commanding

23

general of all forces, Don Jose Maria Ronquillo as inspector general, and Don Donaciano Vigil as acting secretary.

Gonzales called a meeting of all of the influential citizens of New Mexico, including Padre Martinez and Manuel Armijo. He immediately began to take revolutionary measures geared towards the establishment and restoration of good order. They all pledged support to the new government. The new government at Santa Fe denied allegiance to the supreme government (Mexico). They proposed sending a communication to Texas asking for protection [18] if they should be invaded. Texas had won her independence and formed a new republic the year before.

The new military government of New Mexico adopted a tri-colored banner, woven in Chimayo. It had a red band which symbolized the blood spilled by New Mexico's heroes and martyrs in defense of their land; a yellow band, the color of gold, the most noble of metals, that symbolized the elevation of ideals and the nobility of the sentiments that inspired their cause; and a white band representing the purity of the land of New Mexico. The

24

coat-of-arms displayed a fighting cock toying with a snake in its beak. The fighting cock had always been a symbol that was identified with the Hispanic-New Mexicans. It had arisen as such due to the *Corrida del Gallo* and the cock fights that were an integral part of Hispanic New Mexican life.

The fighting cock as a symbol went back into antiquity and was quite popular with heralds. The vigilance and pugnacity of the cock made it a favorite symbol of watchfulness and valor. The fighting cock was also the symbol of strife, quarrels, haughtiness and, most important, of victory because he chose to die rather than yield. One writer said, some regard the eagle as the queen and the swallow or wagtail the lady. He termed the cock as the knight among birds, with his crest for a helmet and his sharp crooked bill for a falchion to slash and wound his enemy. [19]

Upon arriving at Santa Fe, Armijo was completely disturbed at his not being chosen commander-in-chief of the territory. Many prominent citizens from Southern New Mexico resented the fact that the executive branch of the new government was in complete control of Northern New Mexicans. The Southern New Mexicans felt that they had no voice in the affairs of state.

On August 27-28, 1837, there was a meeting of the *asamblea general* (general assembly), presided over by Gonzales. Armijo was present and took part. Others who were present were: Padre Antonio Jose Martinez and Don Juan Esquibel, who, with Armijo, were appointed to draft a statement of the grievances of the people. They were to present the statement to the general government. A report was made, authenticated by Gonzales and signed by him, Jose Maria Ronquillo and Donaciano Vigil, who served as secretary.

A full agreement between the Northern and Southern New Mexicans was never reached at the assembly. A meeting of influential citizens of Southern New Mexico was held at Tome on September 8, 1837. This signaled the beginning of a Civil War in New Mexico. The objectives developed at the meeting were the recapture of Santa Fe from the rebel forces and the declaration of allegiance to the government of Mexico.

An armed volunteer force was placed under the command of Manuel Armijo. The second in command was Mariano Chavez from Los Padillas. The secretary selected was Vicente Sanchez Vergara. The strengths and weaknesses of the "*Canton de la Canada*" (military encampment of Canada) were discussed at the meeting. The members of the committee decided to appeal to the Indians to remain neutral. They declared, the state of war was between the Hispanic New Mexican *rancheros* and they had no intentions of harming or injuring any Indian.

The former Mexican Commanding General of New Mexico, Jose Caballero, issued a proclamation appealing for the support of the Mexican government. He asked for the overthrow of the unrecognized government at Santa Fe. Appealing to the Southern New Mexicans he stated,

> "The whole neighborhood breathes enthusiasm and decision in a cause so sacred, and nothing else is there to wish but the cooperation with the sane and sensible section of the people of Rio Abajo; for so far as regards the people of Rio Arriba, (we cannot count with them now) the truth is that they are in a state of revolution, and we would do them a great injury by believing that a fourth part of them are not in favor of disorder."

Jose Caballero warned the Southerners to defend themselves and form a counter-offensive. He believed that the Northerners were going to put a plan into execution of plundering the territory of the Rio Abajo.

The Alcaldes of the Rio Abajo must have been genuinly inspired by Jose Caballero's proclamation. They soon had the people aroused and thinking of a move to counteract an invasion of the South. A counter-assualt would soon pit brothers against brothers and cousins against cousins in a battle that never touched the magnitude of the American Civil War but carried the same stigma of separatism. General Manual Armijo assumed the command of the volunteer forces and at once set out to liberate New Mexico from the hands of the Northerners.

General Armijo marched into Santa Fe where he discovered that Gonzales had gone. He was informed that the General was in Santa Cruz de la Canada where he was gathering his troops. In a few says the Northern forces would be at full strength at the military encampment. Armijo moved swiftly and made a surprise attack upon the disorganized rebel army. Both armies fought bitterly with many of the soldiers dying in battle. Armijo was victorious. He returned to Santa Fe where at a later time he was notified that the rebel army was regrouping a counter attack.

Padre Martinez used every means of persuasion to keep the revolutionaries from fighting. He was at last able to get others to listen to him. The priest was therefore able to prevent a greater calamity than the one that threatened. As a result some of his own parishioners, persecuted him and he found it necessary to escape to Santa Fe to save his life. Martinez left Padre Lucero to help at the parish of Taos and Picuris. Upon leaving for Santa Fe he had an armed barricade placed in Taos to preserve order. As a result, the rebels did not leave Taos. The priest offered his services to General Armijo at Santa Fe as chaplain of the army.

Manuel Armijo and his troops went out to encounter the rebels which were united in the hills of Puertecito de Pojoaque. He started to arrange his army in battle order. The rebels fired the first shot. At once the General cried "*Arriba*, to die or conquer." After much fighting, the Northerners retreated through the hills and did not stop until they came to Arroyo Seco (about 15 miles to the north). The militia followed them, destroying their outer ranks and leaving dozens dead in the *canadas* and *arroyos* of that sorrowful place. [20]

Jose Gonzales had asked permission to see General Armijo in an attempt at negotiating a compromise. Armijo, however, was very unwilling to make any deals. So he called for the immediate death of Gonzales before a firing squad. He summoned the priest to hear Gonzales' final confession telling him,

"Padre Martinez, hear this genizaro's [21] confession so that he may be shot at five times!"

The leaders of the revolutionary army were ultimately captured and put to death. The battles ended with the defeat of the Northerners. Padre Martinez sent word to Juan Antonio Aragon, Mayor of Taos, of the victory of the Armijo forces in Pojoaque. The situation temporarily quieted down.

The Padre returned to Taos and after hearing that other revolutions threatened, he would try to pacify the unrest. The Northerners felt that defeat was a bitter pill to take, but the priest constantly appealed that their starving families were far more important than the retaking of Santa Fe. The fields had been destroyed first by Armijo's men and then by the Northerners to deprive the enemy of food. They finally listened to Martinez' counsel and laid down their arms. *El Conciliador* continued distributing food from his personal granaries at the church and saved many people from inevitable starvation.

After the pacification of the territory of New Mexico by General Manuel Armijo, his actions were approved by the Mexican government. The Mexican government then reciprocated by changing New Mexico's system of government to that of a *Commandancia* (Commandery) with Armijo as the military governor and commander. His rule was stern at the start, but since he was a native New Mexican, the people accepted him. Armijo later allowed the election of a legislative assembly and here the Northerners found a victory. They won the positions and all of Armijo's moves were subject to their approval. Thus ended the only attempt in the history of New Mexico to establish a locally directed government at Santa Fe as a republic.

Padre Martinez set about to help repair the damages which were the result of war by consoling the families that had lost their sons or father, and providing and caring for the injured, sick, and dying.

Of the five students that had left for Durango late in 1836, two had been initiated into the Orders soon after their arrival. The remaining three students sent by Padre Martinez were taking longer than others. This was due either to the lack of books with which to study, or the fact that they had not begun their studies until November 1834. Two other seminarians at Taos had completed their Grammar and Rhetoric and since May of 1837 had begun taking Philosophy along with Padre Lucero.

Unknown to Martinez, his greatest antagonist was still across the ocean at this time. Jean Baptiste Lamy was ordained in the Mont-Ferrand seminary chapel after studying theology for six years, on the Ember Saturday of Christmas week in 1838. He was then assigned to a small parish at Chapdes in the diocese of Clermont. Lamy and Machebeuf however, were at their respective parishes for a short time. They were enthusiastically interested in going to America. Father Comfe, the Sulpician rector of Mont-Ferrand, received word from Rome from the bishop of Cincinnati, Ohio, John Baptist Purcell. He was returning to Ohio and would go to France on the way, where he hoped Father Comfe would help him recruit young priests. Comfe spoke to five priests including Lamy and Machebeuf who he knew were interested in going to America. They agreed and approval for the journey was obtained from Bishop Feron of Clermont-Ferrand.

Arrangements were made with a certain degree of secrecy since the rector felt that Machebeuf would be forbidden by his father to go to the United States. Machebeuf, under obedience to the rector, departed without notifying his family. His father was angered when he was informed. The five young priests met Bishop Purcell at the Sulpician Seminary of Foreign Missions in Paris. Purcell wrote to Machebeuf's father asking him to forgive his son for his inconsideration. Machebeuf felt great relief upon being forgiven by his father.

John Baptist Purcell was a native of Ireland who in 1818 emigrated to the United States. He began theological studies in preparation for the priesthood. After eight years he completed his studies and was ordained in Paris in 1826. Seven years later he became the bishop of Cincinnati.

The Northern New Mexicans were still unsatisfied with the loss of executive control after the war and they didn't fail in placing the blame on Padre Martinez. Insinuations were carried to such an extent that in 1838 he felt forced to state an account of his merits to date which were related to and written down by Santiago Martinez. The work was titled *Relacion de Meritos del Presbitero*

28

Antonio Jose Martinez.

Before sailing for America on July 8, 1839, Lamy became ill. Machebeuf sent for the seminary doctor who diagnosed that it was just a curious weak spell. Purcell sent Machebeuf without Lamy's assistance to Dieppe to run some errands for him. He returned to Paris a week later finding his companion well and in good spirits. Lamy and the others had spent their days sight seeing in Paris. This had apparently helped to improve his health a great deal. At Le Harve, France, the young missionaries began the journey on July 9th, 1839 because of bad weather. The journey would lead them to the new frontiers of America.

By May of 1839, the Utes and the Jicarilla Apaches led a massive revolt in New Mexico. Padre Martinez was recognized by all Indians as a great holy man. But not even he, could keep them from continuing the revolt. They were temporarily subdued after much fighting and the priest was finally able to settle back fully to the business of his seminary and church.

On August 20, 1839, Purcell and his group arrived in America. In New York, they gazed in awe at the metropolis that was the passage way to a new country and life. The party stayed with Bishop Bubois until the following day when they began their journey inland. The first main stop was Baltimore where they payed their respects to Archbishop Eccleston, the primate. From Baltimore they continued their trip by stage coach to Wheeling, West Virginia. At Wheeling they boarded a steamboat to Cincinnati, arriving there on September 10, 1839.

The missionaries were stationed at a small seminary until they could be assigned to their duties. Everyone at the seminary was too busy to pay attention to them or teach the young Frenchmen any English. They soon became bored with their inaction. Purcell finally decided to assign the missionaries to parishes in Ohio although they needed more training. Father Lamy was assigned to Danville and Father Machebeuf to Tiffin.

In Danville, the walls and roof of the church had been put up but not finished. Father Lamy was quite happy in that some Protestants had helped with the building of the church. His next task would be to build a rectory for himself next to the church.

In 1840, Father Lamy began building a small brick church at Mount Vernon. He could not see his old friend Machebeuf often but they would however, visit in Cincinnati on their visits to the bishop. By 1841, Lamy wrote to Purcell expressing moments of self-doubt saying,

"great deal to be done...if I had only that sacerdotal zeal." The people were having financial problems in the United States, but Lamy obtained the funds for his rectory. It was close to being finished by April, 1841. While the church at Mount Vernon was being built Lamy said Mass in various private homes. Machebeuf was reassigned to Sandusky. His church, a vacant storeroom.

Padre Martinez' relations with the Americans had always been friendly being that he served as their consul. However, he had to attack Charles Bent for his secret association in trying to acquire the Beaubien-Miranda land grant. The head chief of the Taos Pueblo sought the priest's help in putting a stop to it. The land which would be covered by the grant was the communal grazing and hunting ground of the Taos Pueblo Indians.

The huge land grant was to cover practically all of northeastern New Mexico. At Bent's Fort, Padre Martinez made accusations of Charles Bent's involvement in illegal activities. Martinez used all his power and political influence in Mexico City to prevent Bent from obtaining the grant. Charles Bent's hatred and disdain arose because of this. He sought any excuse or opportunity to attack the priest. [22]

On one occasion Bent wrote,

"Back in 1840, Padre Martinez made a trip to Durango, Mexico, and when he returned to Taos his friends and parishioners joyously received him. As was natural, informed them of everything that occurred on the trip and his fine reception which was the object of his journey, etc."

On the 30th of January 1841 he wrote to Manuel Alvares at Santa Fe,

"You asked me for local news of this place. I shall endeavor to give you such as has come to my hearing. The great Literary Martinez since his return has been the all interesting topic. He has been kept constantly employed since he got home, retelling to his greedy admirers and hearers the great respect and attention that was bestowed on him on his last trip to Durango. (Martinez received the position of permanent pastor at the Taos parish.) He says that he is considered by all who he had an opportunity of conversing with, as one of the greatest men of the age. As a literary, an ecclesiastic, a jurist and a philanthropist and more over as he has resided in one of the most remote sections of the province entirely dependent on his own resources for such an emense [sic] knowledge as he has acquired. It is astonishing to think how a man could possibly make himself so eminent in almost every branch of knowledge that can only be acquired by other men of ordinary capacity, in the most enlightened parts of the world but as he has extraordinary abilities he has been able to make himself master of all this knowledge by staring nature in her modest guise. He is a prodigy and his great name deserves to be written in letters of gold in all high places that this gaping and ignorant multitude might fall down and worship it, that he has considered to remain amongst and instruct such a people. It is certainly a great blessing to have such a man amongst us, these people can not help but find favor in this and the other world in consequence of having such a man to lead and direct them: If the days of miracles had not gone by I should expect that God would bestow some great blessing on these people through this great man. And possibly whenever the wise rulers of this land hear of the great fame of this man they will no doubt do something for these people in consideration for the great care of this more than Solomon.

"Ignacio Martinez is here taking depredations, respecting the animals that were stolen from him last season by Juan Nicholas Maestas and party and were afterwards captured by some Shawnee Indians. His object I am told is to try and prove that the animals were purchased by me and my people for the purpose of making me pay for said animals. I am also told that the great Martinez is making him a representation to the Governor on this subject, how true I can not say. If you have an opportunity to mention this subject to the Governor I wish you request him to call on me and such witnesses as I can produce to contradict Ignacio Martinez's statement. But let it be understood that if the said Martinez does not substantiate his statement he must pay all my expenses and those of my witnesses, and if it is to the contrary make me responsible for expenses.

"The chief's of the Arapahoes have made a formal demand through officials of the Mexicans for those prisoners taken by the Eutaws, they offer one horse for each prisoner, and if this is not accepted they threaten to retaliate on these people. I have advised the justice of this place of this demand and that whether any notice will be taken of this I am unable to say. But if they should not heed these Indians they may repent when too late. There are residing with the Arapahoes, one or two Mexicans that are Maes and Anistacio to lead them to any part of this province.

"I had almost neglected to mention that the great Martinez has said that the Texan's have been beaten in Coahuila and California. Wonderful, how did the Texans get there, and where were they going!!! He deserves to be crowned Pope for his geographical knowledge. I think I and Workman will visit Santa Fe next week.

Respectfully yours,
CHARLES BENT"

31

Many writers, in reference to Bent's hatred for the priest, blamed Padre Martinez for the antagonism that existed between Bent and the New Mexicans. But Padre Martinez, as it is known, always sought to help Charles Bent and even performed his wedding ceremony.

The padre's dedication to the community was so pronounced that he opened an orphanage. Many of the orphans were also his students and helpers. Martinez had several acres of land which he and his students cultivated. This was done for their own provision as well as a certain amount which was apportioned for the poor. He raised and instructed the orphans under his care in leading good, wholesome, Christian lives.

On more than one occasion the priest proudly introduced as "his children," his students and the orphans he was rearing, to visiting Americans.

> *"Estos son mis hijos"* (these are my children), he would say, "I educate them, care for them and prepare them for the struggles of life. They can then return home and better serve their families, communities, and New Mexico herself."

It seemed strange to the Americans when the orphans would refer to the priest as "their father." They understood when he explained, he had raised many of them since childhood. Their parents had been killed during Indian attacks upon wagon trains and villages. He also raised an Indian boy that had been abandoned at the Church door. In fact, many had come to him in this manner. The priest throughout his life referred to all, including the Indians and Americans, as *"mis hijos"* (my children).

Lamy and Machebeuf kept up their comradeship inspite of the obstacle of distance between their respective parishes. Father Lamy surprised Machebeuf by paying an unexpected visit to see him begin his new stone church. Machebeuf admitted to his old friend,

> "even if the Devil is often in my purse, I am happy."

Jean Baptiste Lamy was once again suffering from self doubt. Bishop Purcell had become not only his superior, but also the one person Lamy felt he could confide in. In all frankness he wrote,

> "... if I was a priest or minister according to the heart of God, the divine seed would bring forth fruit, though sown by a pour [sic] sower. I beseech you that you pray God that he may enable me to be a good priest, and to persevere in that state, that I may procure the glory of God, and the salvation of those souls which he had redeemed at so great a price." [23]

Texas gained its independence from Mexico in 1835 and declared a republic. After the cessation of hostilities in New

Mexico, Texas turned her sights for a possible invasion of the territory in 1841. News of the impending invasion filtered into New Mexico and Armijo made ready.

He issued a warning to the Americans presently in Santa Fe not to leave the capital. He then issued a proclamation to the citizens of New Mexico asking for their loyalty and patriotism in defense of their homeland.

New Mexicans were a patriotic people and more than ready to fight for their independence. Many volunteered to augment the regular standing army. Battle plans were drawn up and the troops were positioned. Although the Texans had a hard journey in reaching New Mexico, they still felt quite confident that it would be rather easy pickings. But their confidence turned into despair when they encountered New Mexico's defenses. Hopes of victory turned into humiliating defeat. Their chants of "New Mexico and Texas shall be one" died down and the New Mexicans relished their second major victory since the De Vargas Reconquest. General Armijo returned to Santa Fe in herotic triumph, recalling to mind the triumphant returns of Rome's Ceasers after a

conquest. Throngs of people greeted and praised him. Plays commemorating the feat were written and preformed to his and every New Mexican's delight. [24] The event became an annual celebration resplendent with *luminarias, fiestas* and processions.

Father Lamy, by this time had been experiencing financial difficulties with the parishes. He tried to force money problems toward a solution by asking Purcell,

"...there are times which goes very hard with some people of those settlements to help toward the church when some things is to be done, and also to contribute a little according to their abilities for the support of the clergyman in regard to this last point I do not know what to do with a number of them. I wish you would advise me some means to make them do. Could I not tell them, that if they do not help little, even if they are not able to do much, they have no right to the services of the priest? Could I not try to scare some of them refuse to hear their confessions once or twice? You will oblige me very much if you suggest what I could do in such a case..." [25]

He also wrote to the bishop concerning those which he considered to be lapsed Catholics. That is, those Catholics that would fail to attend Mass but would ask for spiritual ministration when sick. Would he be required to administer the sacraments to them? Lamy felt that they would return to their sinful comforts when recovered.

He reported to Purcell,

"These last two months I had some sick calls for some people who were not Catholic, two men married, and a boy of twenty years. They were very low, they have got well; and the poor innocent creatures think my visit did them more good than all the medicines; they now come to church regularly, and I hope, they will be good Catholics..." [26]

Padre Martinez had found an opportunity to convert Americans to the Catholic faith and lost no time in doing so. Many, including some atheists, were baptized by him. And when he baptized their recognized leader, Christopher 'Kit' Carson, whom he had known since 1829, on January 28, 1842, others followed his example.

The Baptismal record of Carson reads as follows:

"Carson, Christopher. In this parish of Taos, on the twenty-eight day of January, 1842, I the parish priest D. Antonio Jose Martinez, after giving the necessary religious instructions and when I was satisfied that he was sufficiently instructed in the principles, the means and the aims of our holy religion, and with his acceptance of the same, and as a reasonable doubt existed as to whether he was baptized or not, since he had been baptized according to the rite of the

Anabaptists, whose errors he abjured—an adult thirty-two years of age—I exorcised him, I anointed him with the sacred chrism, giving him the name of Christopher, the same name which he had received at his first Baptism according to the above mentioned rite. But, the Baptism which I administered to him was according to the Church rite for adults as required by the Roman Ritual: the said adult came from the State of Missouri of North America; but is a well-known fact that even since he was fourteen years old he has lived here in this town, of this parish of Our Lady of Guadalupe, and that he has been engaged in the occupation of hunting in the North: he said his parents were of legitimate marriage—Linsey Carson and Rebecca Robinson: the god-parents were Louis Lee and Maria de la Cruz Padilla, residents of this town, of Our Lady of Guadalupe Parish, whom I instructed in their obligations and spiritual relationship, and in testimony of which I have signed my name. ANTO. JOSE MARTINEZ.''

Shortly thereafter, the priest married Kit Carson to Josefa Jaramillo and in time baptized their children, Teresina, Kit Jr., and Josefita. The priest's conversions were not limited to Americans for he had been converting Indians from the beginning of his ministry.[27]

Padre Martinez served as a representative or delegate from New Mexico to the general Mexican National Congress at Mexico City from June to December, 1842.

Lamy again turned to his bishop in friendship. He had been struggling to try to learn English. He asked Purcell if he would approve of his writing in the new language. But this was not problem enough. He was to face yet another language difficulty. So many Germans were entering into the territory that he wrote,

"one thing is wanted for me, it is the german language, and though I speak but very little English, could I speak the dutch so well, it would be very good.''

About the work he was doing at the missions, he wrote,

"Perhaps I ought to be blamed to do so much in these hard times. in this case I beg your pardon but I do hope good intention will be some excuse.''

He felt great comfort in being able to write to Purcell in confidence,

"It is to you, Revd Bishop that I must open my heart. You have always been a father to me, and I bless the divine providence that I am in this diocese" and "I have the honour to be your devoted child, J. Lamy.''[28]

The problems with the wild Indian tribes in New Mexico had continued to fluctuate throughout the years. It was a constant concern for the priest. He went to the aid of the people, including the American settlers, by writing a report to President Antonio Lopez de Santa Anna concerning the situation. It was published as the "*Opusculo*" on November 28, 1843.

He received congratulations from the president for his concern for the welfare of all the people. He assured the priest that he would look into the matter. Following his work on the "*Opusculo*" Martinez limited his activities due to physical exhaustion. He published a volume on civil rights which bore the same title.

Padre Martinez' younger brother Pascual had since grown into manhood. He had become very attached to his elder brother, especially after their father's death. Martinez' mother had also died by this time. Don Severino had given the list of his children in the order of the oldest to the youngest; Antonio Jose, Maria Estefana, Juana Maria, Jose Maria de Jesus, Jose Santiago, and Juan Pascual Bailon, "youngest of all."

Two of the brothers received the Baptismal name of Jose. Padre Martinez received it as a middle name. The priest was christianed Antonio after his father. Jose Santiago, who married Teodora Romero, was confirmed Antonio. Both Jose 'Antonio' Santiago and Juan Pascual Bailon were married to girls named Teodora, which also caused a great deal of confusion with later writers.

His brothers, Santiago, Jose, and his sisters had married and they all had large families. Martinez was especially fond of his many nephews and nieces and educated some of them at his school. Pascual went on to distinguish himself under General Armijo and eventually became a captain. He fell in love with a young girl from Taos name Teodora Gallegos whom he married. She and Pascual had many children. A daughter of Jose Antonio Santiago also provided a great deal of comfort for Padre Antonio. Many times, he would come to tears reminiscing of his own deceased daughter.

There was a striking family resemblance between Pascual and Father Antonio. More pronounced than that between he and the other brothers and on more than one occasion people confused them at first glance. This was especially prevalent among the Americans who were unaware that there were two brothers that strongly resembled each other. Their resemblance went on to confuse many for years to come even after the death of the priest.

In October of 1843, Machebeuf received word that his father was quite ill. He requested permission to go to France to be with his family but it was denied. The reason given was that no other priest could replace him in Sandusky during his absence. Lamy journeyed to Sandusky to try to console his dear friend and found him grief stricken. Bishop Purcell finally gave permission for Machebeuf to leave for France. The condition being that he recruit new priests for Cincinnati. He was able to leave in June of 1844. It would be a year before Lamy could see his companion again. By May 4, 1845, Machebeuf was on his way back to America. His father had died before Machebeuf had an opportunity to see him. He recruited four priests for Purcell. He was also able to recruit a Father Penderprat to help him out in Sandusky.

By 1845, Padre Martinez was once again selected to serve in the Departmental Assembly.

In July of 1845, Bishop Zubiria returned for another visitation to New Mexico and by the 12th of the month, visited Padre Martinez. The bishop had found even more *penitentes* and asked that all the priests read the decree he had written in 1833 against the brotherhood. Zubiria was again much satisfied with the priest's work and praised him for his humanitarian efforts.

As a result of New Mexico's revolt against Mexico, Deputy Martinez introduced four measures to the New Mexican Departmental Assembly on January 5th, 1846:

"1. That they ask the Supreme government to declare that all offices in New Mexico, both political and military, should be assigned only to natives of the Department.

"2. That the military force be sufficient in itself to cope with the dangers (Indian raids, etc.).

"3. That articles of consumption available be appropriated for aid to the New Mexicans whenever performing military service.

"4. That New Mexico might have an independent treasury (*caudal propio*) from which to pay their employees and other expenses." [29]

It was also decided at the Assembly to ask,

"The Sovereign Congress to grant New Mexico half of the revenues corresponding to the nation." [30]

The answer from Mexico stated unequivocally,

"The state of ignorance prevalent in this territory (New Mexico) makes these free institutions, in which a great portion of the common welfare has been vested by law, useless and of no significance."

On January 13, 1846, the New Mexican Departmental Assembly voted in favor of the formal change of the territory of New Mexico. The change was from that of a Department to an independent *Commandancia General*, apart from the fifth division of the national territory of Mexico.

By April of 1846, by legislative edict of the Departmental Assembly, the priest received authority to act as a lawyer in civil affairs. Up to this time, the clergy in New Mexico had been prohibited from participating in civil law.

The tide of Manifest Destiny would change the New Mexican scene. News of another invasion crept into New Mexico. This time the threat was from a much more formidable opponent that would test New Mexico to the core. Armijo would have his third trial. His first two had been great victories. He had put down a rebellion and repulsed an invasion.

General Armijo called for volunteers. He issued a proclamation and called for New Mexican patriotism to defend their land against American imperialism.

General Armijo appealed to President Santa Anna and the Mexican Congress for additional aid. He was certain it would be a matter of time before it would arrive. Appeal after appeal went unanswered and the grim reality arose that aid from Mexico would not be forthcoming. He called his military council and civil council to a meeting. As could be expected he found traces of unwillingness to fight. The reasons: the useless shedding of blood; they felt it was inevitable that the United States would send larger and larger armies to take over; New Mexico had been in a state of semi-independence during the Spanish rule, this became the same under Mexican rule and who was to say it would not remain the same during American rule? After all, what difference would it make if one flag was changed for another at the palace? Mexico itself lent a deaf ear and seemed to abandon New Mexico. New Mexico had just been over an internal revolution likened to a civil war. The New Mexican troops fought against the New Mexican liberation armies. Also, they had adequately prepared themselves against a Texan invasion. New Mexico was war weary and the treasury insufficient to equip even a minimal defense.

A vote was taken and the question settled. Kearny's forces would be allowed to enter without firing a shot. Armijo bitterly opposed the decision and continued with appeals to opose the American entry.

In a meeting of the departmental assembly held late in June by Manuel Armijo it was stated that he:

"Informed this illustrious corporation of the urgent circumstances in which the department finds itself placed, upon which the enemy of the national integrity is now advancing, and therefore he sought as is clearly a matter of imperious necessity that the representatives of this body be summoned so that, without the loss of a single moment, they may present themselves for the discharge of the duty entrusted to them and that so this corporation may decree measures in accord with their prerogatives. The governor's wish being taken under consideration, it was agreed without discussion to proceed at once to dispatch the communications indicated, which same were immediately addressed to their honors: Jose Chavez, Antonio Jose Martinez, Manual Gallegos, and Juan Perea, requiring them that, without excuse or any delay whatever they present themselves in this body, the two first on the ensuing Friday, July 3rd, at 9 A.M., His Honor Senor Gallegos on the morrow at 4 P.M., and His Honor Senor Perea on the same day at 10 A.M.; with the understanding that in case they fail, this illustrious assembly will make them bear the consequences to which they may make themselves liable as a result of failing to comply with the decree of this body. F. Sena; Jose F. Levba, Antonio Sena.''

Governor Armijo sent a message to Colonel Pascual Martinez (brother of Padre Martinez) on July 11, 1846, in order to arrange for a meeting to discuss the crisis that was developing. Attached to it was a list of men he should take along. The message read as follows:

"It is positively known that the forces of the United States which it is announced are coming to take over this Department, are on the march and in order to consult with the most influential sons of the country as to the means we should take for our defense, I instruct you within three days after receipt of this message to present yourself before me bringing with you those citizens named in the list attached who under no pretext will be excused for we are to discuss the welfare of the Department or of its lost cause which should interest all of us. God and Liberty!"

The list: Antonio Jose Martinez, Don Blas Trujillo, Don Juan Vigil, Don Cornelio Vigil, Don Buenaventura Martinez, Don Carlos Beubien, Don Jose Maria Valdez, Don Mariano Lucero, and Don Eulogio Valdez.

During a meeting of the assembly held on July 13, 1846, Manuel Armijo informed them of Kearny's advancing forces. At the meeting Don Tomas Ortiz offered the following resolution:

"Excellent Sirs: I ask the illustrious assembly, in view of the urgent circumstances in which the department finds itself with regard to the foreign aggression, that the executive governor and commanding general of the same be empowered to take all those measures which may seem proper for the conservation of the national territory whether it be that they tend to securing extraordinary provisions to maintain the forces or that they be of such character as not to allow of any ordinary resolution, said license to his excellency to last until

39

the end of the war."

A vote was taken and the resolution failed.

On August the 9th, 1846, a special session of the Departmental Assembly was held at the palace of the governors, at which time the majority of those present declared in favor of not fighting. The assembly held another meeting on August 10, 1846, in which Armijo asked for a sum of money then equivalent to $1,000 to maintain his forces. The assembly then authorized a forced loan on the public credit. On August 11, 1846, they cancelled the appropriation and revoked Armijo's authority to collect. This was the last official act of the Departmental Assembly. One that points out the dire circumstances under which Armijo was operating at the time.

A report written by one James Magoffin to the Secretary of War of the United States government on August 26, 1846, states:

"I arrived at Bent's fort on 26 July, where I found General Kearny, presented the letter I received from your hands, and was well received. The General on the 1st of August, dispatched Captain Cooke with 12 dragoons, accompanied by myself, with a letter to Governor Armijo, which was delivered of 12th instant 10 o'clock P.M. We were well received and dined with his Excellency. Had a long conversation with him and proved to him from General Kearny's letter that the troops entering the Department were only to give peace and protection to the inhabitants, and assured him that I had been dispatched by the President of the United States in order to inform him and the rest of the good people of New Mexico with whom I was acquainted that this was the only object of our government. I found many of the rich of the Department here, also military officers, with whom I had ample intercourse. I assured them the only object of our government was to take possession of New Mexico, as being a part of the Territory annexed to the United States by Texas and to give peace and quietude to the good people of the country, which gave them entire satisfaction."

During the course of the discussion, Armijo mentioned that he would send a commissioner to meet General Kearny. The General declared that he personally would lead a force of six thousand to meet him.

On August 14, 1846, General Manuel Armijo made his last will and testament, proving that he was preparing to meet the enemy in battle. He was resigned either to die on the battlefield or be captured and taken prisoner. As will be seen by the will, in such an event he felt it necessary to be ready for a defeat, or more optimistically, a victory:

"Let it appear by these presents, that I authorize with sufficient general power Don Gaspar Ortiz, in case of death, or during my absence, to settle all private affairs with as much power as if my affairs were his own. He is authorized to deal and contract in my affairs, and in the event of the death of my wife before me, he shall remain in charge of all my interests without there being anyone to hinder him in the exercise of his duties until he disposes of the same, as my last will. The civil judges will honor this extra-judicial document as if it had been executed with all the solemnity and necessary legal clauses and provisions required in law. He has been given my instructions for the distribution of my fortune in whom and in the best manner possible without any abatement whatever, settling my testamentary with sufficient power. MANUEL ARMIJO

"To this frank manifestation of my sentiments is witness Don Donaciano Vigil, Santa Fe, August 14, 1846."

Also on August 14, 1846, General Kearny received a message from General Armijo which stated:

"You have notified me that you intend to take possession of the country I govern. The people of the country have risen en masse in my defense. If you take the country, it will be because you prove the strongest in battle. I suggest to you to stop at the Sapello and I will march to the Vegas. We will meet and negotiate on the plains between them."

General Kearny chose to disregard the message and continued to march.

Unknown to General Armijo, James Magoffin had been carrying on a policy of subversiveness. In regards to his own men, Magoffin succeeded in obtaining the support of Colonel Diego Archuleta, second in command to Armijo. Colonel Archuleta had been placed in charge of setting up the defenses at Apache Pass. He was to make preliminary preparations before the arrival of Armijo and the remainder of his troops. Archuleta went about the business of undermining the entire military operation and coercing the forces into mutiny. James Magoffin wrote of the event in his report to Secretary March:

"Was then assured by Colonel Archuleta, second in command, that he would not oppose General Kearny's entrance. General Armijo on the 15th ordered his troops, say 3,000 in number, to be placed between two mountains, with 4 pieces of artillery on the road by which our army had to pass. Having promised General Kearny to have an interview with him in his note borne by Captain Cook 14th inst., say some 50 miles distant at a place called the Vegas, Armijo left this place

(Santa Fe) early on the 16th with 150 dragoons and joined his army, called his officers together and wished to know if they were prepared to defend the territory. They answered they were not, that they were convinced by the proclamation that they had seen from General Kearny that the United States had no intention to wage war with New Mexico, on the contrary promised them all protection in their property, persons and religion. Armijo, apparently appeared very much exasperated, gave orders for the troops to be dispersed and in 48 hours they were all at their homes, he himself leaving for the state of Chihuahua, with say 100 dragoons, maltreating all good citizens on his route and pressing their animals."

Armijo had appealed continuously for assistance from the Assembly, but the northern New Mexican dominated body denied him any help. The members of the assembly had been assured by American envoys that they would remain in control. Some even felt that conditions might even be better under the United States government.

General Stephen Watts Kearny and his troops arrived as weary and forlorn as the Texan invaders. They expected resistance but found none. The streets were relatively empty except for a planned reception when they entered Santa Fe. The proclamation was read. The United States stars and stripes were raised in a bloodless change of governments. Now August of 1846, New Mexico had become an American possession.

Armijo's cabinet met with surprise when questioned about not putting up a fight. The explanation:

"Well, uh, the traitor Armijo. Oh yes, the traitor Armijo absconded with New Mexico's treasury and deserted us. We were left without a leader so what were we to do?"

American officials saw an opportunity to discredit New Mexico's courageous hero for fear of his return. The people could find a cause and appeal to him for a revolt. It was common knowledge at the time that Armijo could easily incite and organize a quick offensive. The Americans were not about to take chances with any inclination on his part on doing this. Armijo was also considered to be a military genius that had aptly proven his ability on the battle field. He became an outcast in his own land. He was independently wealthy but his purported thievery and treachery was readily accepted.

General Armijo, after the war, was tried in Mexico City for cowardice and desertion in the face of the enemy. After all of the witnesses were summoned and the developments leading up to the occupation were throughly investigated, Armijo was acquitted of all charges. [31]

Don Diego Archuleta went on to distinguish himself in the service of the *United States government*. Armijo, who did all he could to try to stop the American takeover and defend New Mexico, has been described as a traitor. Armijo's treatment as a traitor has cost New Mexico dearly, with the loss of a truly heroic figure.

Padre Martinez himself had long since become familiar with the United States Declaration of Independence and the Bill of Rights. The principles espoused by both documents were the same as those he had held sacred from the beginning. By the time of the American entry, he was totally in favor of the democratic principles of the United States and accepted the change of government. Padre Martinez was among the first to pledge allegiance to the new government, and many followed his example.

Father Penderprat who was brought from France to America by Machebeuf to assist him in Sandusky, was assigned to Louisville by Bishop Purcell. The counties in Northern Ohio were growing faster than the others. All Machebeuf could do was to continue complaining of having more work than he could handle. The American bishops decided to petition Rome to divide the area of Cincinnati and create a new diocese. Purcell proposed Father Rappe, who had come to America along with Lamy and Machebeuf, as the bishop-designate. This would mean that Sandusky and Danville would be included in the new diocese under Rappe. Machebeuf again said he was desperate for help. Purcell then decided to send Lamy in late August of 1846 to Sandusky to help Machebeuf. Lamy replied,

> "Everybody, except in my own congregation knows that I am going to Sandusky City...one thing only I regret it is to be cut off from the diocese of Cincinnati." [32]

Sandusky was described as a city filled with every imaginable vice. It was stated that "dreadful scenes" went on in the public streets. Drunkenness and street fights were a daily happening and even reached the church doors.

Lamy wrote to Machebeuf in September to say that Bishop Purcell had unexpectedly felt obliged to change his decision. Machebeuf unhappily wrote to Purcell. He did not now know how he could single handedly change the civil disgraces and the religious neglect which brought ill repute against the Catholic Church in Sandusky. Machebeuf was also displeased in that he had not been invited to attend the consecration of Bishop-designate Rappe.

The same month also brought bad news to Lamy. His father had died in Lempdes on September 7, 1846. Father Lamy wrote to

Purcell that his family,

> "urge me very much to go to France, but I have no desire of going...(He asked the bishop to) be so good as to pray for the repose of his soul."[33]

Relations between the Americans and the New Mexicans declined soon after the occupation. The New Mexicans resented the military government that had been imposed in Santa Fe. They repeatedly asked, that a civil government be set up. Kearny's promise that New Mexico's leaders would remain at the head of the government did not materialize. Some of the former leaders of the Departmental Assembly (excluding the priest) organized a revolt.

Diego Archuleta was named commanding general. The revolutionary armies were organized at lightning speed. Ironically, ten years after the first major revolt in 1837 against Mexico, a second attempt at taking Santa Fe was under way in 1847. This time it was to take control away from the Americans rather than the Mexicans.

The Indians again became a major factor in that they joined the Spanish New Mexicans in the revolt. And, as history repeats itself, the governor, Charles Bent, and several other Americans were slain by the Indians as they had done with Perez and his group. The families of the Americans sought refuge at the home of Padre Martinez after the initial attacks. He was awakened from a restless sleep. A multitude of people were at his doors crying,

> "Open for the love of God! Open for us! The Indians are killing Charles Bent, Louis Lee and others!"

The padre hurried to the door letting the people enter. They were desperate from fright and terror. He provided food and refuge for everyone. [34] Padre Martinez had long been aware of the rumblings of discontent. But he had begged restraint and counselled everyone to wait for the organization of a civil government to state their grievances.

Turbulence clouded New Mexico's skies. Skirmishes and several major battles were fought by Americans against newly formed New Mexican liberation armies. The liberation armies were finally subdued. The leaders faced the firing squad or the hangman. Colonel Price, the Military Commander, as Armijo before him, gave no quarter to the enemy. But in contrast, Armijo was condemned for his actions, Price was lauded for his. Many of the rebels were hung for treason against a country in which they were not even citizens. The American presidency later declared, the rebels were not traitors but true patriots fighting for their homeland against a military occupation. They were, therefore, to be regarded as New Mexican heroes and not as anarchists.

44

Kit Carson returned to New Mexico with the intention of murdering Martinez. Many had wrongly accused the padre of having been one of the conspirators of the revolt. After speaking to his wife, Josefa, and the others that the priest had saved, Carson changed his mind.

In December of 1847, Padre Martinez continued his leadership role amongst the New Mexican people. As a representative in the legislative branch of government, he headed a petition in favor of annexation to the United States. The opening statement read in part,

"...New Mexicans, not through fear, but for the sake of their well-being, avail themselves of the opportunity to seek the good will of the American government of the north...(asking) ...to be numbered among its citizens, with all the privileges and rights awarded to its people."

The next few years were busy ones for Padre Martinez. They were spent in attempting to reunite his people. The new era was soon to become the most crucial for the Padre, and one which would test his inner strength and endurance to the core. New Mexico itself had been involved in two revolutions, a civil war, the repulse of the Texan Invasion, and the American entry. All occured within a period of ten years, 1837 to 1847. It had been too much.

In Sandusky, Machebeuf's parish grew even faster. In February, when Lamy and some other priests went to Niagara Falls, Machebeuf could not go along. He could not afford the trip and, besides, had too much work to do at his parish.

Rome decided that the creation of a new diocese in Cincinnati was not needed. This proved to be an embarrassment for Father Rappe, the bishop-designate.

In July of 1847, Lamy received distressing news. Central Ohio was not growing very fast. Bishop Purcell decided to move Father Lamy to Sandusky permanently where help was needed. Lamy wrote a long plea to be allowed to remain in Danville. Telling Purcell,

"If I was to consult my taste I should be obliged to say that I have a great dislike to be charged with the cure of a community on account of my inexperience and of my age for I am only thirty-two." [35]

Lamy pleaded,

"please bear with me a little longer. You have too great idea of my capacity as far as I know myself I would be afraid to exercise the ministry in a town or city. You might be too much disappointed in your expectation, if there is a certain good done where I am, though only a little, suffer me to remain here.''.[36]

Purcell finally agreed not to send him to Sandusky.

In August, Jean Baptiste Lamy took out his United States citizenship. Bishop Purcell decided to assign Father Lamy to Covington, Kentucky. On August 20, 1847, Lamy wrote to Purcell that he would be glad to go there and said,

"One thing which consoles me is to know that I will be so near you..."

Lamy's assignment to Covington, Kentucky would be directly across the river from Cincinnati, Ohio.

Rome eventually approved the new diocese and Father Rappe was consecrated. Lamy shortly after being assigned to Covington made plans to go to Europe to settle his father's estate.

On the 10th of October, 1848, as a result of the New Mexican revolt, a convention met in Santa Fe with Padre Martinez as president, and J.M. Giddings, as secretary. Other members of the convention were Elias P. West, Antonio Saenz, Juan Perea, Donaciano Vigil, Santiago Archuleta, Francisco Sarracino, Gregorio Vigil, Joseph Pley, James Quin, Ramon Luna, Charles Beaubien, and Manuel A. Otero. The convention submitted a memorial to Congress asking for the establishment of a civil government.

When all indications of war between the United States and New Mexico were over, Padre Martinez was able to continue his dedication to the priesthood. His little church and seminary at Taos were once again beehives of activity.

In July of 1848, Father Lamy returned to his native France. Arriving in Lempdes he negotiated with his brother, Etienne, concerning his father's estate. Lamy said,

"My brother has not been so hard to deal with as I had expected."

He was also able to visit with his sister, Margaret, who was now a nun of the order of Misericorde at Riom. She wanted to go off to America with her brother upon his return trip. She wished to be dispensed by her superior so that she could join the Brown County Ursulines in Kentucky. On receiving the approval, Margaret and Lamy's niece, Marie, joined him when he set sail for his return to the United States.

While Lamy was in France the question arose again as to whether or not he should be assigned to another parish, probably in the Cleveland diocese. Bishop Rappe's answer to Purcell,

"I feel more inclined to let everything in status quo."

Lamy returned to Covington. He went to visit Machebeuf in Sandusky. They had many things to discuss. Lamy brought back some items that Machebeuf had requested that he obtain for him during his stay in France. Unfortunately, Lamy forgot the two items he needed most, two white dalmatiques.

During the month of May of 1849, the American bishops gathered in synod at Baltimore. The church officials discussed the problems they had with the acquisition of the Mexican territory to the United States. It was generally believed that the area was in a dormant religious state. Truman Smith, the Congressman from Connecticut, had already stated in Washington that the land was,

"under the control of the clergy to an extraordinary degree. The standard of morals is exceedingly low...the country is little better than a Sodom...I am free to say that if all the vices which can corrupt the human heart, and all the qualities which reduce man to the level of a brute, are to be 'annexed' to the virtue and intelligence of the American people, I DO NOT DESIRE TO BELONG TO ANY SUCH UNION."[37]

The bishops gathered at Baltimore felt, the territory was in need of immediate attention.

The Synod made several requests to the Pope. The bishops asked for three additional archbishoprics: New York, Cincinnati (Purcell), and New Orleans (Blanc); eight new dioceses: Savannah, Georgia, Wheeling, West Virginia, St. Paul, Minnesota, Monterey, California; and two vicariates: the Rocky Mountains with J.B. Miege as vicar apostolic and New Mexico with Jean Baptiste Lamy as vicar apostolic.

On July 19, 1850, Pope Pius IX established by decree the vicariate apostolic of New Mexico and on July 23 issued a papal bull naming as its vicar apostolic Father John Baptiste Lamy, of Covington, Kentucky with the title of bishop of Agathonica. His selection for the newly established vicariate of Santa Fe set the stage for his meeting with the "old priest of Taos."

PART II

THE CONFLICT

By 1850, other conditions, primarily the religious change, endangered the traditional religious patterns of the Spanish-speaking residents of New Mexico. This cultural challenge turned many New Mexicans in upon themselves for spiritual comfort. [38] Padre Martinez took up the standard in the struggle to preserve the Human Rights of the people of New Mexico. The struggle matched the priest with the Frenchman turned American, Jean Baptiste Lamy.

The young Frenchman first appeared on the scene as an obscure priest of St. Mary's Parish in Covington, Kentucky. He was elevated to pastor within a short time, and even more rapidly was being considered for the position as Vicar Apostolic of New Mexico.

After the American takeover of New Mexico, civil affairs had changed, but the religious convictions of her people remained as strong as ever. The American Bill of Rights expressed freedom of religion and to New Mexico religion meant life itself.

In 1849, the Mexican bishops had consulted Rome in question as to their continuation of ecclesiastical control over territory ceded to the United States. They were informed that it was their duty to continue to exercise episcopal authority over the area.

Bishop Zubiria returned on an Episcopal visitation in 1850 to New Mexico, to assert,

"although the government had changed, his Diocesan authority had not."

On September 6, 1850, Zubiria, through Padre Martinez' recommendations, announced that the priests should not enter into any agreement with their parishioners as to church contributions, but should accept them voluntarily. After spending six months in New Mexico, the bishop returned to Durango. He had left the priests confident that he would not fail them in his continued administration of New Mexico.

In spite of this knowledge on the part of the American bishops they assembled in synod at Baltimore, Maryland, to recommend to Rome that a new vicariate be established in New Mexico. Europe at this time was going through a political upheaval and Pius IX was in exile at Gaeta. His government had been overthrown and his papal army was defeated by a revolutionary movement. He was later restored to office by French troops.

The council developed an appalling picture of the deplorable spiritual conditions of the newly acquired territory. Stories about the immoral priests' lives were singled out from soldiers reports. It was pointed out that the Bishop of Durango was responsible for the religious conditions of New Mexico in that he had made only three visits there.

The council concluded that the territory of New Mexico should be regarded as missionary ground, ripe for a new church movement. The claims were substantiated with accounts written by American Army officers. They told of the supposed low morality, rampant prostitution, the drinking, gambling, dancing and every imaginable vice amongst the people and religious leaders.

On his return to Rome, Pope Pius IX established by decree the vicariate apostolic of New Mexico. A few days later, on July 23, 1850, the Pope named Father Jean Baptiste Lamy of Covington, Kentucky as vicar apostolic with the title of Bishop of Agathonica, in *partibus infedelium*. The Church authorities of the See of Durango were, however, not notified.

Father Lamy at first was reluctant to go to such a place. Only three years earlier, Lamy had written concerning his transfer, as an assistant pastor, to a larger town,

"I have a great dislike to be charged with the cure of a community on account of my inexperience..."

The new vicar apostolic sought out all of the available information he could on New Mexico. None that he spoke to had any firsthand knowledge of the area. Lamy had to rely on written accounts which were mainly reports made by soldiers that had accompanied Kearny's forces. The accounts informed him that New Mexico's populace was composed of savage Indians and bararous Mexicans.

One such report stated,

"They pertinaciously cling to the customs of their forefathers, and are becoming every year more and more impoverished...- in short, they are morally, physically, and intellectually distanced in the great race of improvement which is run in almost every quarter of the earth. Give them but *tortillas, frijoles, and chile colorado* to supply their animal wants for the day, and seven tenths of the Mexicans are satisfied..."[39]

The people were described as illiterate, primitive in their religious beliefs and uncivilized.

Other Americans entering New Mexico took time out to write about their beliefs about the land and people. One Easterner reported:

"Another evidence of the Catholic Church in New Mexico was

51

the attendance at Mass of devout women, of whom not one was supposed to be virtuos."[40]

American soldiers were certain that all of the native women were primarily prostitutes. Of the religious leaders in the territory one observant American wrote,

"the priests of New Mexico were noted for their corruption and profligacy, and instead of being teachers in morals they were leaders in vice. Their lascivious pleasures were quite as public and notorious as their priestly duties, and there was hardly a priest in the country who did not rear a family of illegitimate children..."[41]

On second thought, Lamy envisioned himself as a great missionary on the way to taming a wild and ruthless frontier. It was a great task indeed, but in his mind he thought of the benefits such an undertaking would bring. His future on the stairway of success was very bright.

On his appointment, Lamy wrote to Machebeuf,

"They want me to be a Vicar Apostolic, very well, I will make you my Vicar General, and from these two Vicars we'll try to make one good pastor."[42]

Machebeuf,

"felt 'neither the necessary talent nor the courage, nor even the patience' for the move.'[43]

And besides, Machebeuf explained, he had finally gotten things settled down in Sandusky. His painstaking efforts were now bearing fruit. Lamy reminded him of their boyhood pledge that they would never be separated. In the past, each had taken turns as the follower and leader with Machebeuf usually assuming the leadership. This time it would be Lamy the leader and Machebeuf the follower. He decided to go along and assist Jean Baptiste in New Mexico.

The next step was to make the journey to Santa Fe so that Vicar Apostolic Lamy could declare his ecclesiastical position. Lamy had discovered that there were two ways of traveling to the Spanish colonial city. One was the much easier route usually taken by traders on the Santa Fe Trail. The trip on the trail would be a much shorter journey. But rash Lamy decided in favor of a lengthier and harder journey taking more than twice the amount of time to reach his distination. Blanc in writing to Purcell was filled with disbelief in that the new Vicar Apostolic would use such a complicated means of travel to reach Santa Fe.

Jean Baptiste Lamy was consecrated on November 24, 1850 at St. Peter's Cathedral in Cincinnati. Lamy had been preparing himself for the consecration since the summer at the nuns convent in Kentucky: The cathedral was generally recognized as an ecclesiastical capitol. Purcell's church was referred to as the "bishop factory" by the clergy. St. Peter's was one of the most beautiful and elaborate churches in America. Lamy's sister and niece both attended the three hour consecration ceremony.

Bishop Blanc of New Orleans and Bishop Purcell of Cincinnati along with the bishop of New York had also been raised to archbishops by the Vatican in 1850. Much to Lamy's disappointment, he would no longer be under Archbishop Purcell but would now be under the jurisdiction of Archbishop Blanc of New Orleans.

Lamy left on November 25, 1850 from Cincinnati on a trip to New Orleans accompanied by his sister and niece. He had already been advised by several to go to Europe first. This would allow Rome enough time to notify ecclesiastical authorities in Mexico of the change. Bishop Rappe added also, he should "seek after new priests who knew Spanish." Blanc also felt that Lamy should go to Europe first, one of his reasons being that he could learn the Spanish language which would enable him to communicate with the Mexican people. Machebeuf also, could not leave as yet, due to his settling of affairs at his parish. They planned to meet in New Orleans and then proceed on the journey. On arriving at New Orleans, Marguerite had to be placed in the Sisters of Charity hospital since she was extremely ill. Lamy's niece, Marie, was placed in the school of the New Orleans Ursulines.

Vicar Apostolic Lamy stayed with Archbishop Blanc at his home. Blanc began to question the impropriety of Lamy's proposed route to Santa Fe. Bishop Odin of Texas had written to Blanc offering his suggestions as to Lamy's trip. He, through experience, knew what the vicar could expect. He added,

"I am an old enough Texan to predict great fatigue and many obstacles on his hard journey, and whole-heartedly wish him a good and heavy purse..."[44]

Lamy's plan was to travel through the Gulf of Mexico by ship to Galveston, Texas. He would then continue on to San Antonio then El Paso past present day Las Cruces and Albuquerque with arrival at Santa Fe. Lamy booked passage on an Army ship free of charge after arrangements with the commander. He would have to leave without Machebeuf. He, however, missed the departure of the ship and decided to sail on the steamship Palmetto. Vicar Lamy left a letter for Machebeuf to follow and meet him in San Antonio. Lamy's sister was now gravely ill at the hospital but he felt, by all means, that he should leave in haste. Unknown to him, the Palmetto had already been condemned as an unseaworthy ship.

By January 8th, 1851, Lamy arrived at Galveston, Texas and met Bishop Odin. He told him of his plans of hurrying to Santa Fe, making a brief appearance and leaving for Europe to recruit priests upon whom he could count. Odin felt, Lamy should first secure the aid of trusted missionaries to help him against the "scandalous" native clergy. Bishop Odin also counselled him to procure new vestments to replace the "rubbish" he would find in New Mexico. Odin felt that the churches of New Mexico were filled with "filth." The bishop of Texas had always had to use his own vestments whenever he had occasion to say Mass there, in place of the torn, soiled ones offered to him.

Bishop Odin felt that Lamy could try to learn Spanish while in France so that he could converse in the native tongue of the people. He could also give Bishop Zubiria an opportunity to notify the clergy himself. Lamy, however, was inclined to follow his original plan. Before their departure, on the evening of the same day, Bishop Odin gave Lamy episcopal administration of Socorro del Sur, Isleta del Sur and San Elizario near El Paso del Norte to help him begin his diocesan duties.[45] Odin informed Lamy, he would send a written account to Archbishop Blanc of the advice he believed should be followed by the new Vicar Apostolic. He would also request that the Archbishop send Lamy to Europe if he agreed with his suggestions.

Lamy departed Galveston on the S.S. Palmetto headed for Matagorda Bay. On January 9, 1851, the sea was tormented by violent storms. As the ship neared the port of Matagorda Bay it passed through a shoal and struck bottom. The Captain maneuvered the ship back to the open sea then made another attempt to cross over the shoal. He failed but he made several other attempts until the hull burst open in a furious explosion that sent water inundating her lower deck. Life boats were lowered and the shipwreck survivors were able to reach the beach. When an accounting was made of passengers and crew members it was discovered that no lives were lost. Practically all of the baggage and supplies did however, go down with the sinking Palmetto. A trunk which contained some of Lamy's possessions was sighted and saved by a strong-armed Negro. The passengers and crew were rescued from the beach and taken to Indianolo. There Lamy would be able to join a merchant caravan to San Antonio.

Joseph Projectus Machebeuf in the meantime had arrived in New Orleans and read all about the shipwreck of the ill-fated steamer. Marguerite who had become steadily weaker had died on January 9, a day after her brother had left. Machebeuf left immediately for San Antonio. Upon his arrival in the Texas city he found his companion bed ridden. He would be unable to move for two months. Machebeuf questioned Lamy as to how he had come to be in this condition. The new vicar apostolic had a curious tale to tell.

After arrival in San Antonio Lamy had gone off to buy a wagon and mules to pull it. He knew they would need such a vehicle to travel on the rough trail inland to Santa Fe. While awaiting Machebeuf's arrival he had decided to make religious visits to the outlying Army posts. On one of these visitations the dragoons left without him on their return to San Antonio. The soldiers were traveling too far ahead for the slower wagon. Lamy then decided to try to catch up. He whipped the mules repeatedly until they took off in a furious run. Lamy was most certain that the wagon would overturn so he jumped for his life. He hurt his leg on landing and was found lying on the ground by a passerby. He was then taken to the city to recuperate from his injuries.

Bishop Odin heard of Lamy's second misadventure and promptly wrote to Archbishop Blanc. A priest of Cincinnati wrote to Archbishop Purcell,

"...Lamy has made a disastrous beginning to his labours..."[46]

Purcell was in Rome at the time.

Lamy and Machebeuf often spoke of the work they were to do on their arrival in New Mexico. "A cathedral must be built," was the first thought. One that would be large and grand in style and rival those of beloved France herself. They would have to recruit French missionaries to help them with the work of bringing the people back into the fold. Yes, there was much to do, but they saw and knew they could do it. Although they did not know the language of the people, they felt that surely many of them must have learned some English by 1851. If they had not they could find an interpreter until they could learn the language themselves.

While Lamy was in San Antonio, he decided to write on April 10, 1851 to Bishop Zubiria. He would inform the bishop of his appointment as Vicar Apostolic of New Mexico. Bishop Odin again wrote to Blanc giving a report on Lamy on May 13, 1851. Several more days passed before Lamy and Machebeuf were able to join a group of two hundred wagons towards New Mexico. They lost no time on the trip reaching San Elizario, Socorro, and Isleta in June of 1851.

Lamy was received cordially but found great difficulty in trying to lay claim to the three towns as a part of his new vicariate. He was informed that Bishop Zubiria only and not Odin had jurisdictional authority over that particular area. The area, in reality, belonged to the diocese of Durango and the creation of the new vicariate apostolic of Santa Fe would not affect it. Zubiria had given charge of the three towns to the pastor in 1849. He had received orders from the Vatican to do so. All were unaware of

Bishop Odin's disposition of administerial duties to Lamy. This went on to plague him with a jurisdictional confusion for years to come.

Lamy arrived in El Paso, Texas, on his way to New Mexico where he met the pastor, Ramon Ortiz. The priest recommended that Lamy should write of his appointment to church officials in New Mexico. Lamy did so immediately. While in El Paso he observed that the churches could have been better kept. The new vicar apostolic believed it would take him time to know more about the customs and practices of the people in regards to religions. He had already learned that violence and vice was commonplace in El Paso. The *fandangos* (local dances and social gatherings), it was felt by Americans, provided the setting for licentious acts amongst the Mexicans. In writing to Archbishop Blanc, Lamy stated his fears that Santa Fe might be the same and from what he had heard, he was sure of it. [47]

Lamy and Machebeuf, as they advanced on to Santa Fe, passed through several towns with parishes every fifteen to thirty miles. Upon seeing the churches and the people, they became convinced, the religious devotion and piety which was shown them was only superficial. The blame, it was felt, could only be attributed to the native clergy. Lamy felt that the local priests were either lacking in zeal or were living scandalous lives. Yes, the people went to Mass, had their religious sodalities and kept the feast days, but, for the most part they failed to keep the sacraments. [48]

Vicar Juan Felipe Ortiz had received the word of the coming of an American who alleged to be the new vicar apostolic of the vicariate of Santa Fe. The news was met first with disbelief and then with amusement. *Es imposible!* (It's impossible!) they thought. Ortiz decided to meet the vicar and find out what this was all about. He and a few others rode out to await Lamy's arrival. Lamy wrote of his reception,

"Senor Vicario (Vicar Juan Felipe Ortiz) of Santa Fe came to wait for us a hundred miles from the capital.' [49]

Early on Sunday, August 9, 1851, Lamy and Machebeuf arrived in Santa Fe after a journey which took more than eight months.

Things were quite different in New Mexico from what Lamy and Machebeuf had imagined. The Mexican clergy was well entrenched. Vicar Juan Felipe Ortiz stood at the head of the Church, next to Bishop Antonio Laureano Zubiria, whose Episcopal seat was in Durango, and second to Vicario Ortiz was the Very Reverend, Antonio Jose Martinez. [50]

The clergy ministering in New Mexico for the Mexican period of the Church until Lamy's arrival in 1851 included : (1) Fray Teodoro Alcina, (2) Padre Jose de Jesus Cabeza de Baca, (3) Padre Manuel

Bellido, (4) Padre Juan Caballero, (5) Fray Benigno Cardenas, (6) Fray Jose Castro, (7) Padre Rafael Chavez, (8) Padre Vicente Chavez, (9) Padre Jose Manuel Gallegos, (10) Padre Ramon Antonio Gonzales, (11) Padre Francisco Hurtado, (12) Padre Jose de Jesus Leiva, (13) Padre Mariano de Jesus Lopez, (14) Padre Mariano de Jesus Lucero, (15) Padre Jose de Jesus Lujan, (16) Padre Antonio Jose Marin, (17) Padre Antonio Jose Martinez, (18) Fray Diego Martinez, (19) Padre Manuel Martinez, (20) Padre Ramon Medina, (21) Padre Francisco Minguez, (22) Padre Fernando Ortiz, (23) Padre Jose Ortiz, (24) Padre Jose Eulogio Ortiz, (25) Vicario Juan Felipe Ortiz, (26) Fray Rafael Ortiz, (27) Padre Jose Antonio Otero, (28) Fray Jose de la Prada, (29) Padre Manuel de Jesus Rada, (30) Padre Geronimo Riega, (31) Fray Jose Francisco Rodriguez, (32) Fray Jose Rubi, (33) Padre Antonio Jesus Salazar, (34) Padre D. E. Salazar, (35) Padre Ramon Salazar, (36) Padre Jose Mariano Sanchez, (37) Padre Juan Tomas Terrazas, (38) Padre Juan de Jesus Trujillo, (39) Padre Eulogio Valdez, (40) Padre Nicolas Valencia, (41) Padre Manuel de Valle.[51]

As many as thirty seminarians were instructed at the Our Lady of Guadalupe Seminary at Taos under Padre Martinez. The young men were eventually ordained and assigned throughout New Mexico. The priest's school was growing annually. New students were being recruited throughout the area. Those that were ordained and working at their respective parishes sought wholeheartedly to search for new candidates to the priesthood.

Lamy and Machebeuf were astonished when Ortiz and his priests demanded to see their papers. They examined the papers carefully and found none from the ecclesiastical authorities of the See of Durango. They refused to acknowledge Lamy and Machebeuf until they were notified by their bishop to do so. They stated with good reason, they had received no communication from Mexico concerning any such change and they were still bound to their superior, Zubiria. Lamy and Machebeuf withdrew to confer about the situation. It was then recalled what others had advised from the beginning. Lamy wrote to Zubiria asking for a swift confirmation by letter of Rome's new appointment.

While in Santa Fe, Lamy decided to take custody of the military chapel, *La Castrense*, which had served Spanish, Mexican and later, American soldiers. The popular chapel had been erected during the Spanish Colonial era strictly for military use by the government. Lamy, in his desire to secure a base, sought to take over the chapel. He met stiff opposition from the United States Supreme Court Chief Justice, Grafton Baker. Baker contended that precedence established it as governmental property and brought it automatically under United States jurisdiction. He was pressured by other Americans to let the bishop have a base of operations as an antidote to the native clergy. Baker relented with Lamy's promise that he would repair and restore the Spanish Colonial chapel.

Lamy reinstituted the tithing that had been removed by the previous government. The Mexican clergy had exercised a powerful influence over the people's temporal interests. The result was that the clergy had imposed the mandatory payment of enormous tithes for the ecclesiastical acts of their ministry. They had exorted the tithes with rigidity and without mercy. Many times the poor had to bury their dead in the deserts; leave their little ones unbaptized; and live in concubinage if unable to pay for the marriage. There were those who stole to pay the tithes and the courts were full of such cases.

Padre Martinez recognizing that such burdens, instead of edifying the faithful and promoting the well being of society, only served to corrupt the Christian citizen. He wrote a treatise in which he denounced the results of such abuses. Public sentiment was aroused and the Federal Mexican Congress withdrew the civil obligation for the payment of tithes to the clergy in 1833. [52]

On August 28, 1851, Padre Martinez wrote to Zubiria in regards to the situation in New Mexico. He stated his regrets that the area was no longer under Zubiria's jurisdiction. The priest said, hard times had befallen his people. The padre also wrote about the announcement of the tithes collection and their remittance, which troubled him. He also mentioned, New Mexico was going through a severe drought. Locusts plagued the crops. The crops had been reduced to a tenth of the expected yield.

Lamy's general opinion of the Mexican homes was that they resembled mud houses; of the churches he observed that they reminded him of nothing more than the "stable of Bethlehem." *La Castrense*, he felt, was adequate. Santa Fe as a whole was "uncivilized." When a *fandango* was held, it seemed as though the dancers went from the dance to early Mass, followed by the same musicians that played the same tunes for funeral, dance, and Mass.[53] In writing to Paris twenty days after his arrival in Santa Fe Lamy wrote concerning the native clergy,

"...there were 15, 6 of whom are now old...even now they are either incapable or unworthy..."[54]

He made a report to the Society for the Propagation of the Faith at Lyon. In his census of the Catholic Church of New Mexico, Lamy stated he found sixty eight thousand Catholics, two thousand "heretics," and close to forty thousand "infidels." He also added that their were eighteen missions, twelve native priests, twenty-six churches and forty chapels. In a letter Vicar Apostolic Lamy wrote,

"The state of immorality in matters of sex is so deplorable that the most urgent need is to open schools for girls under the direction of Sisters of Charity." [55]

He also appealed for zealous French missionaries that could help him with the situation. To Purcell he mentioned,

"On my arrival in New Mexico I found frightful abuses among the clergy."

The Society for the Propagation of the Faith felt that Lamy's statement of the church in New Mexico was insufficient. They went on to ask him to submit a,

"True statement of these missions." [56]

Lamy was finally forced to travel to Durango in September, 1851. He had not as yet received an answer to the letter he had written to Zubiria. Lamy's rejection by the native clergy made him more determined as he traveled southward. The offended vicar apostolic painted the scene of his rejection in his mind over and over again. No power on earth could keep him from reaching his destination. After a five-week journey ended, Lamy asked to see Bishop Zubiria.

Jose Antonio Laureano Lopez de Zubiria y Escalante had already been the bishop of the See of Durango for twenty years when Lamy arrived to see him. He had been born in Sonora, Mexico in July of 1781. Zubiria was highly regarded for his austere dedication to his duties. He was also noted as a careful and thorough prelate. But where he could be stern in his administration, he could also be kind and understanding with the people and priests in his diocese. He and the other Mexican bishop that had diocese' that crossed over into what was now territory of the United States, had been ordered by the Vatican to continue their authority over the area. The only notice Zubiria had received of the newly created Vicariate Apostolic of Santa Fe was through the letter from Lamy.

Bishop Zubiria and Lamy conversed in Latin during the course of their discussion. The bishop stated, he had answered the vicar's letter on June 12th. Zubiria went on to say, he had not been notified by Rome concerning the change. He had written a letter of protest to the Pope concerning his receipt of notification from the Vicar Apostolic rather than from the Holy See. He felt, this could not be regarded as official notification. The elder bishop believed, Lamy should have gone to Rome to make his duty to the Pope. Official notification could have then been sent to the bishop in authority and preparations made to receive the new Vicar Apostolic in New Mexico.

Lamy presented the papal document which showed that the

Vicariate Apostolic of Santa Fe had been created. Zubiria then responded,

"I knew nothing about it officially, but this document is sufficient authority for me and I submit to it."[57]

With Lamy's complaint of the insubordinate clergy, Zubiria affirmed that his priests were entirely within their rights in not transfering allegiance without his instructions.

Bishop Zubiria wrote a letter to the Vatican while Lamy was in Durango. The letter dated November 1, 1851 would inform church officials of what had transpired during their discussion saying,

"I, the present Bishop of Durango, Jose Antonio de Zubiria-Escalante, as hereafter subscribed, owing to the honor of my having as the guest of my house the Illustrious Lordship Don Juan Lamy, Bishop of Agathonica in *partibus infidelium* and Vicar Apostolic appointed for the territory of New Mexico, by our reigning Pontiff, the Supreme Bishop Pius IX, may whose reign be long and filled with God's blessings, for, since God possesses all power and facility to do so, may he so deign; and, since, assuredly, God will so do; and whereas such concepts being clothed as they are with mere words, and these are so susceptible to change and variance within the human intelligence of mankind: obviously, then, despite this frailty of human communication, I have no choice accordingly but to accept this medium through which to express my message, and it is thus written as follows..."

He stated he would,

"recognize as of now, as Vicar Apostolic of New Mexico, the said Illustrious Lordship Don Juan Lamy."

He also gave orders for the clergy under his authority to submit to Lamy. Zubiria asked that the limits of his own diocese be defined. The American bishops were trying to lay claim to an extensive area into Mexico, past the border of the United States. The Mexican bishop maintained that this could not be done. Lamy was generally in agreement (in the future he would argue about his "rash" decision in Durango). The bishop also questioned as illegal, the transfer of the three border towns by Odin to Lamy. Rome had not authorized any such transfer and they remained under the Bishop of Durango. He did add,

"should there come to me, by some legal way, other information referring to the said cession of the above mentioned places, be it for the authority of the Bishop of Texas, or be it to New Mexico, it shall be done."[58]

Vicar Juan Felipe Ortiz arrived in Durango to consult with the bishop. Zubiria explained the matter to his vicar and asked that he transfer his allegiance to Lamy. He was also told to notify the clergy and laity of New Mexico concerning the transfer. He was to make the change as easily as possible. Lamy, assured of no difficulties and wished success by the bishop, returned to New Mexico.

Bishop Zubiria received an answer to the first letter he had written to Rome. The Pope officially informed him of his decree on November 12, 1851.

Machebeuf, while in Santa Fe, was invited to say Mass the following Sunday by the parish priest, Padre Jose de Jesus Lujan. He spoke to the congregation but none understood what he said. After Mass they all wondered as to what religion the stranger might belong.

> "He must be a Jew or a Protestant," said some, "Because he does not speak as Christians do... *Quien sabe?* (Who can tell?")[59] replied others.

New Mexico's priests, in the meantime, felt quite confident that the foreigner would not return. They, and the people that had heard that a new vicar apostolic had come, were after all quite sure that he was anything but, a Catholic dignitary. Since the American takeover, many Protestants and Jews, and *"quien sabe que"* (who knows what else) were among the newcomers.[60]

Lamy reached Santa Fe on January 10, 1852 armed with Zubiria's authorization. He was certain that he could not rely on any native priests in his entire diocese. He had referred to them in the past as being either "incapable or unworthy."[61] He had urged several pastors to "mend their ways."

The native priests acknowledged Lamy's authority after seeing Bishop Zubiria's letters which declared that Durango no longer held jurisdiction over Santa Fe. Lamy, in a letter to his former superior, wrote,

> "They showed me good face, though I have reason to think they will submit rather by force than by good will."[62]

He had found that the priests exercised a great deal of influence over the people who were reluctant to accept him. He entertained hopes that many of the native clergy would leave and if they so did, he wished them Godspeed, being that,

> "they are more in the way than help."[63]

He suspended one of them, the pastor of Pecos, because he had supposedly gotten drunk on a Sunday night, had fallen from his horse and broken a leg. Lamy confided to Purcell,

> "There are several other cases in which I might use the same severity, but still, as they have not been caught in the act, I must wait with patience, and try at least to keep them under fear."[64]

Several of the New Mexican priests chose to work in the Durango diocese rather than serve under the new foreign vicar apostolic of New Mexico. Lamy also wrote, he felt

"obliged to go very slow, and to be very prudent..."[65]

The native priests, he believed, exercised "great influence."

On February 5, 1852, Lamy journeyed through several towns in New Mexico. He observed, for the first time, the native folk art that decorated the churches and missions. It was obvious that Lamy and Machebeuf would have a personal dislike for the native craft.

While Lamy had been in Durango he left Machebeuf in charge of collecting money. He had collected enough funds for *La Castrense* and repairs had commenced. Lamy had intentions of bringing nuns to New Mexico and beginning a school. He found a home which could be used to house the sisters, but it belonged to "a rich Frenchman." Although it would be an expensive matter to buy it, he would let Machebeuf handle the negotiations. Machebeuf was uncertain how he could collect the monies but he would have to find an answer. He purchased the home for sixty-five hundred dollars.

The vicar apostolic would have to attend a council to be held at Baltimore by the bishops. Lamy left Santa Fe to attend on April 1, 1852. On May 9, 1852, the council held a session wherein they decided to ask the Pope to elevate New Mexico to an Episcopal See and raise Lamy to bishop. The area would then fall under the jurisdiction of the Metropolitan church of St. Louis. If His Holiness granted their wishes then Lamy would not be subject to decisions made in Durango in regards to boundaries. They might also be able to obtain control of the three border towns. The council concluded its business on May 20th, and the final resolutions were signed by thirty-two bishops.

Lamy extended his trip to include a visit to his niece, Marie. He was also able to obtain some nuns to take back with him to New Mexico. The group accompanying Lamy had a hard journey on their trip to Santa Fe, arriving on September 26, 1852. Machebeuf had much to tell Lamy about the native priests.

On September of 1852, Lamy removed two more priests, Jose Manuel Gallegos of Albuquerque who had been a former seminarian under Padre Martinez and D. B. Salazar, pastor of Santa Clara.

There were as many as thirty young priests that had attended his seminary at Taos and had received Holy Orders.[66] In fact, the priest still continued sending candidates for ordination after Lamy had arrived in 1851. He had also continued recruiting the native youth for a vocation in the priesthood.

While on a trip to Santa Clara, Machebeuf had accused Padre

Salazar of drunkenness and adultery. When not receiving any answer to the charges, Machebeuf reported the incident to Lamy. The priest was promptly suspended by Lamy. The Vicar Apostolic then encountered an additional problem. He had no one to replace Salazar with in Santa Clara. Machebeuf was sent to reinstate the suspended priest. Before returning to Santa Fe he felt that he should remain to hear how the priest conducted Mass. Salazar commerced the *Te Deum* with words that shocked Machebeuf,

"O God, sustain my cause; give me redress against a race that knows no piety; save me from a treacherous and cruel foe."[67]

Padre Salazar was immediately suspended a second time.

Gallegos had been completing arrangements for a journey to Durango while Lamy was absent on a trip to Baltimore late in 1852. Gallegos had however, received permission from Machebeuf to make the trip. He delegated his church duties to Padre Lujan. Lamy returned before Gallegos' departure, but he left as planned. Machebeuf informed Lamy that he had given Gallegos permission. Lamy felt that Gallegos should still be suspended. He believed that the priest was going on an unlawful trip to Durango. Lamy immediately sent Machebeuf to take charge of Gallegos' Albuquerque parish. He was to publish a decree of suspension against the absent priest by saying, he had not received permission from the Vicar Apostolic to make the trip.

Machebeuf then ordered Padre Lujan to leave the parish of Albuquerque. He would take care of church affairs there as he was able to. Lamy suspended Lujan for two years. The charge being that he had been living with a woman. The priest answered in his defense. Lamy was forced to reinstate him because the priest at Pena Blanca had died and he was again faced with the problem of a replacement. Father Machebeuf himself was being accused at Pena Blanca of neglect in his priestly duties.

Padre Martinez wrote to Lamy stating, he had violated Canon law with the suspension of Gallegos. Nine hundred and fifty of Gallegos' parishioners sent a petition to Lamy in his defense, stating that he had gone to Mexico on important business with Bishop Zubiria. The parishioners complained that with the removal of Padre Gallegos and Lujan, they had been left in spiritual abandonment. Father Machebeuf made infrequent visits to the church. Because of this neglect, many of the dying went without the last rites and others were left without the sacraments. The parishioners went on to say that Machebeuf, while at the church, had been threatening denial of the sacraments to those who did not pay the tithes. It seemed to the parishioners that

Machebeuf always ended the Mass with "the private lives of the Faithful."

Lamy's problems with Gallegos remained but he would have to turn his attention to the immediate problem at hand. The question of the tithes was at the forefront of his difficulties. Although the priests received voluntary support for their parishes, it was not enough for Lamy to put his plans into operation. He had many ideas which he said would be to the people's advantage. What had been given voluntarily would have to be made an obligation. Lamy decided in favor of issuing a pastoral letter to be read in all of the churches. It would also be printed in the *Gaceta de Santa Fe*, the Santa Fe newspaper. This, he hoped, would be the answer to his problem. The pastoral letter appeared before the public eye on January 1st, 1853.

The letter listed the following regulations which would be effective immediately on the first of the year, 1853: all services provided by the ministers would remain the same except that Mass would only be held once a month (as compared to once a week as done previously) in chapels that were at a distance not more than three miles from the parish church, these chapels would also have to have at least thirty families in attendance; all pastors were to collect the tithes, keeping only one fourth and the remainder sent to his office in Santa Fe; candles would not be required in any of the services. The faithful were instructed to obey the Church in all that was asked. It was also mentioned that many had met their obligation during the past year. He wished that he would not be forced to impose severe penalties for the disobediance of those that failed to comply. Those that continued in their disobediance would not receive the sacraments and they would be considered as being outside of the fold.

Lamy reproached the people by warning that their immoral ways could only lead to divine punishment. Of the *fandangos* (dances) he stated, they were conducive to evil, occasions of sin, provided opportunities for immoral relationships that were reprehensible and sinful. He likened the dances to a school of immorality and vice. In his estimation, all New Mexicans who attended the profane diversion had lost their fear of God, their innocence and honor. Saying,

> "Be not deceived, neither fornicators, nor adulterers, nor highwaymen, nor those given to drinking nor blasphemers, nor thieves, shall inherit the kingdom of God..." [68]

Upon reading the blanket reprimand of the people, Ortiz ordered Lamy out of his home, where he had been staying. Lamy maintained that it was church property. Ortiz, stating that the land and home were his personal property, presented the deed to prove it. He had made the purchase of the land from Bishop Zubiria. There was a stipulation that the land and home which Ortiz would build would revert to the church only upon his death or resignation as vicar at Santa Fe. Lamy then attempted to divide the Santa Fe parish of which Ortiz was the *Parochus Proprius* (irremovable rector) to assume control.

Many of the parishioners went to the aid of Ortiz. Machebeuf referred to them as being, "most of them corrupt in every aspect." Lamy then decided to take control of the lower part of the parish and use *La Castrense* as his church. His only recourse would be a lawsuit to obtain the disputed property.

Other priests objected to the pastoral letter and division of the parish of Santa Fe. Some refused to read the letter to their parishioners and were suspended. Padre Jose de Jesus Lujan (the Santa Fe priest transfered to Pena Blanca) was ordered directly by Lamy to read it to the parishioners. The padre openly refused and was promptly suspended of all priestly duties. Two other priests, Padre Jesus Baca and Padre Antonio Otero resigned after receiving the pastoral letter. Lamy gave them a month to reconsider. After not hearing from them, he formally suspended the priests.

The rumblings of protest began to surface and increase rapidly. The discontent was being voiced strongly by the people themselves.

The parishioners from the Pena Blanca area strongly accused Machebeuf of neglect and an obsession with the collection of the tithes. He was also accused of revealing the secrets of the confessional, which had it been any other priest, would have brought about his immediate expulsion.

They were also very upset in that Machebeuf spent very little time in Pena Blanca, reporting to Lamy, he
> "is no sooner here, than he is already in Taos, Mora, San Miguel, Albuquerque, or elsewhere."

They complained that they were left without any spiritual ministration. When Machebeuf was in Pena Blanca it appeared as though he was only interested in money.
> "as if this was the only obligation for the faithful."

He was only concerned enough to
> "reveal the secrets of the confessional."[69]

Machebeuf described his accusers at Pena Blanca as
> "all kinds of savage animals, who work only for their temporal life and not for spiritual ends."[70]

The residents of Pena Blanca asked for a resident priest, adding
> "we do expect Your Lordship to seriously consider this, our just application, even though the information possibly might

be disagreeable to him."[71]

However, Lamy considered it a personal affront and asked for proof concerning the allegation which had taken place during his absence.

Lamy wrote on January 14, 1853,

"It is necessary to see what kind of defense he (Machebeuf) can make in his own behalf, since such matters are of themselves so very grave that they would seem to require juridical proof; and until such time as I am given proofs of what lies behind your demands, I shall consider the presentation as a calumny of the most malicious kind that could ever be made against the character of any priest; and accordingly, it shall be my duty to punish such persons who have made such accusations. Adios! Your friend and Vicar Apostolic, Juan Lamy."[72]

In reference to the required proof, Lamy asked for the answer to the following questions:

"First, when and where was the violation of the seal of the confessional made?; second, to whom was it made?; third, what things were revealed?; fourth, the name of the person whose sins were thus revealed? Send me the answers, with proofs, as soon as possible. Adios."[73]

Before receiving such proof, Lamy wrote to the accusers that Machebeuf could justify himself once the proof was submitted. Considering the case closed he asked that they refrain from meddling with the operation of his administration.[74]

Lamy began a primary school for young boys which was operated by some Lorettine sisters he had brought to New Mexico. Some of the children of wealthy Americans and New Mexicans began to attend the school. But the Hispanic-New Mexicans were penalized for speaking Spanish in school. All of the parochial schools in New Mexico, from then on, made it mandatory to use English, although New Mexico was regarded as a bilingual territory.

With the return of Padre Gallegos on March 1, 1853, the parishioners of Albuquerque begged for his reinstatement and the removal of Machebeuf from the Parish.

In response Lamy answered,

"the rehabilitation of Father Gallegos will be very difficult indeed, at least for now, because he did not obey my orders during my absence, and furthermore, he left his parish without the permission of his superiors. (Meaning himself even though he was not around at the time and had left Machebeuf to take his place at the time of his absence. Machebeuf had given Gallegos permission.) As for the

67

removal...let me tell you this: that is my business alone, and I myself will decide what is to be done about the errors of which you accuse him (Machebeuf). At the same time, let me give you some advice in all charity: that you ought to adhere closely to Ecclesiastical Authority; otherwise, you place yourselves in the gravest of difficulties." [75]

There was a lapse of a few weeks before Lamy received a letter from Don Ambrosio Armijo, the probate judge at Albuquerque. He had represented the petitioners of the Albuquerque parish at San Felipe and was once again writing for them. The parishioners, Armijo wrote, were shocked that Lamy would attempt to

"intimidate them with threats of future difficulties, in order that they should now begin to keep the necessary silence."

The parishioners at Albuquerque, as in Pena Blanca accused Machebeuf of breaking the vow of the secrecy of the confessional. The accusation was quickly overlooked by Lamy. He stated, if what they said was true, then how was it that Machebeuf had long lines of people at the confessional. He, however, disregarded the fact that Machebeuf was the only priest available in several of the churches because their pastors had been removed. Also, during the Christmas season it was a custom for all to go to confession.

Padre Gallegos returned to Albuquerque from his trip to Durango and went immediately to the rectory at San Felipe de Neri Church. Machebeuf quickly sent a message to Lamy saying that he needed a document to confirm the suspension of Padre Gallegos and assertain that he, in fact, was now in charge of the parish. On the subsequent Sunday Machebeuf read the letter of the suspension of Gallegos at the church. Padre Gallegos, rather than answering impulsively at the moment, left. Machebeuf was ordered out of the church by the parishioners some days later. He was, of course offended, sending for the municipal prefect to have them arrested. By the time the prefect arrived the parishioners had gone, Machebeuf dropped the charges.

Lamy had proceeded with the division of the parish of St. Francis at Santa Fe. Padre Martinez along with Vicar Ortiz, Padre Gallegos and Lujan signed a letter written to Lamy protesting the division. Ortiz decided to leave Santa Fe on a trip to Durango to confer with Bishop Zubiria. Before leaving, the vicar stated to Lamy in no uncertain terms that he would inform the Pope of what Lamy was doing in New Mexico. Vicar Juan Felipe Ortiz would not return to the New Mexico scene for another two years. The main reason being that he became ill while in Durango.

Vicar Apostolic Lamy decided to make the church of St. Francis his cathedral abandoning *La Castrense*. The church of St. Francis (popularly referred to as *la parroquia*) was completed soon after

1714 after having been rebuilt. The last stage of the rebuilding was the finished north chapel which would house the statue of *La Conquistadora*. It was the principal church of the capital and served as the main church for Vicars San Vicente, Rascon and later Juan Felipe Ortiz.

The large building had two chapels in the crossing, one with the advocation of Our Lady of the Rosary and the other with that of St. Joseph. The statue of Our Lady of the Rosary, known as *La Conquistadora* is believed to have been brought to New Mexico by Fray Alonso de Benavides. It was carried to safety by the retreating Spaniards during the terrible Indian revolt of 1680. It was returned to Santa Fe during the Reconquest by General Don Diego de Vargas. The statue now had a permanent home in the north chapel of the *parroquia*. One of the side chapels had a door connecting it with the cloisters and dwellings reserved for the religious serving the administration of the capital.

Lamy continued having troubles with the parishioners at Pena Blanca. Don Francisco Tomas Cabeza de Baca represented the families and once again he wrote to Lamy although he had been told,

> "Now permit me to inform you that when it will be necessary to write me, I will so advise you. I will have great pleasure in receiving any of your letters, please write in an easier style." [76]

DeBaca wrote to Lamy questioning the suspension of Padre Lujan without proof. Adding that he felt Lamy had done likewise with others of the native priests.

Lamy's reply:

> "I don't remember having given you offense on any occasion; and I hope that from now on you will not oblige me to instruct you as I have...I can assure you that I don't have any resentment against you, but I believe you have written as you have under some sort of presuppositions." [77]

The Vicar Apostolic believed that de Baca should not have accused him of suspending the priests without the required proofs. Lamy was certain that he had reason enough.

De Baca again made the original accusations against Machebeuf. He stated that Machebeuf was also denying the sacraments to the parishioners. In regards to the "easier style" of writing he said,

> "I will never be able to use any other kind of writing." [78]

De Baca informed Lamy, his letter was

> "written without any kind of persuasions."

Again, De Baca wrote to Lamy telling him of what had happened, quoting Machebeuf's words on his last visit to Pena Blanca.

Machebeuf had become angered when told that the citizens would further pursue their claims against him. He declared,

"Since you want to threaten me with presentations to the bishop, let me tell you this, that he and I grew up together; that we were ordained together; that we have missioned together in the United States; and that he knows me well, and this for many years; and as a consequence, the Bishop never does anything without first consulting me..." [79]

According to De Baca, Machebeuf had attacked all of those in attendance at Mass, even the ones that had not signed the petition against him. It was announced by De Baca that Machebeuf had talked about a ten year old boy, about a man living in a state of adultery with his sister-in-law, and about a man that had not gone to confession for an unimaginable eight years, during the sermon. Machebeuf could happily report, he had absolved their sins and restored them to grace. He made it very obvious at the sermon who was being spoken about.

Lamy was informed that if the case of Machebeuf's betrayal of the confessional was not heard, then,

"we shall have to appeal to higher powers, in behalf of the faithful whom I might have to represent." [80]

Lamy, by this time had already received complaints from the people of Albuquerque and Pena Blanca of Machebeuf's betrayal of the secrecy of the confessional. Now he received a letter from Padre Martinez making the same accusations against Machebeuf. Lamy showed the letter to Machebeuf. Machebeuf immediately wrote to Martinez. He said, all that he had found out in the confessional which he had discussed had already been learned in every day conversation, sometimes in the presence of others, and was common knowledge. If the people already knew anyway, what had been confided in the confessional and he let them know he was happy these sinners had come to grace, then he was not the first to divulge the information. Martinez then wrote to Lamy saying, he was satisfied with Machebeuf's answer. Also that Machebeuf in his sermons appeared to "annoy and bother his hearers" although he regarded himself as "very persuasive." If he were "more moderate in his approach, according to the ordinary rules of oratory" he might produce "the necessary good fruits or results." [81]

Machebeuf continued saying Mass once a month in Albuquerque, Pena Blanca, Santa Clara and some of the other towns. In the meantime, these towns were without parish pastors. Lamy tried to borrow two priests from Purcell. Purcell was, however, unable to comply.

Several native priests held a meeting against Lamy. They sent him a letter, which four of them signed, stating they would henceforth consider null and void any act of his administration. They also mentioned their intention of appealing to the Vatican. Lamy immediately appealed to Purcell to help him by countering whatever might be sent to Rome by the New Mexican priests.

In writing to Cardinal Barnabo, Prefect of the Sacred Congregation of the Propaganda Fide in Rome, he said,

"I thought it prudent to inform your Eminence on this matter, so that if their complaints ever reached the Holy See, you would be informed already, and from a good source, as to how these things happened, and that the critical circumstances I was in and the abuses I witnessed obliged me to be severe and to interpret the ecclesiastical law in favor of order and religion."[82]

Lamy also wrote to the Primate at Baltimore, Archbishop Kenrick repeating what he had told Purcell and Cardinal Barnabo. Kenrick wrote in Lamy's behalf to Rome. He used what Lamy had informed him of

"as another reason why there should be created an Episcopal See in the city of Santa Fe..."[83]

The United States bishops finally won. On July 29, 1853, Pius IX raised Santa Fe to the full status of a diocese. The bishops could now work on changing the boundaries, although Lamy had made an agreement with Zubiria in August of 1851.

Before Santa Fe was raised to an Episcopal See, Ortiz in Durango, had sent documents to Rome describing Lamy's actions in New Mexico. Archbishop Clementi, the Apostolic Delegate at Mexico City had delivered the papers for Vicar Juan Felipe Ortiz in Rome.

Padre Martinez had made several trips to Santa Fe. He had gone to receive the new Vicar Apostolic and at other times to offer his help, assistance, and advice. Martinez was suffering from poor health and could not make trips to Santa Fe as often as he would have liked to.

Lamy continued his tithing. By this time the diocesan collection amounted to eighteen thousand dollars a year. Even the non-Catholic settlers from the East felt that his tithing was an offense. The poor people could not make their payments to the Church and were being penalized.

Trouble at Pena Blanca again surfaced when several of the people became adamant in their refusal to pay the tithing. Don Francisco Tomas Cabeza de Baca, to whom Lamy had written before about accusations against Machebeuf, received a letter from Lamy which said:

"Dear Sir: having been informed by one of my collectors that you have as yet not completely paid up the different parts which correspond to tithing, it is now my duty and obligation to inform you that as long as you obstinately refuse to pay your just debts, I cannot allow any priest whatsoever to celebrate Mass in your private chapel at Pena Blanca."[84]

In answer to Lamy's letter Baca wrote:

"Monsignor: I have before me your note of the 17th of the present month of May, and so in adequate response, let me say to Your Lordship: that it is now and will be my firm resolve not to pay any kind of tithing fee, as long as it is demanded of me as some sort of contract payable by me for spiritual administration, the present powers of which may well be within the powers of a Catholic bishop; and this being so I see no reason to worry about the same; since, for over a year now, we have been given bad administration; [Machebeuf had been saying Mass once a month; he had betrayed the secrecy of the confessional; if someone died he would have to be buried without services.] and so I now beseech and even advise you, first to consult what you owe to your own conscience, for I suspect there is some prejudice in Your Lordship against my own family. Therefore, let Your Most Illustrious Lordship quit your vengeful censures. Though you use such reprehensible means to force me to make you plans effective, first with your now usual threats, and then later with your denial of spiritual ministration, [anyone that did not make their payments to the church were denied the sacraments and were considered outside the fold] such procedures, let me inform Your Illustrious Lordship, don't impress me in the very least; not only because of the notorious injustice which the Monsignor habitually uses in these serious matters, but also because the sheer mercy and piety of all Christians do not depend on the blatant use of absolute power that your Lordship commands, as I've learned from others of the Faithful in New Mexico."[85]

Pope Pius IX had created on Episcopal See in the city of Santa Fe on July 29, 1853. Now, for some strange reason, there was a question as to who had become the actual bishop of the newly created diocese. A leading newspaper in Ohio, the Cincinnati *Catholic Telegraph*, carried the significant news that Santa Fe had been raised to an Episcopal See. The newspaper had the shattering report that the new bishop of Santa Fe was [not Lamy] Don Juan Felipe Ortiz. The article added that he had been Vicar at Santa Fe for many years.

Could such an announcement be correct? It was true that Lamy had only been vicar apostolic for less than two years. Whatever the case, Lamy lost no time in having an article printed in the Santa Fe

New Mexican on December 3, 1853, stating that he was, in fact, the bishop of Santa Fe.[86] The matter was, for the moment, apparently over.

The people of New Mexico had the yearly custom of holding a novena in honor of the Blessed Virgin Mary. The celebration was held in December during the Christmas season. Machebeuf had a personal dislike for such festivities in that he believed, the local people used such events as opportunities for "dances," and "orgies."[87] Lamy allowed Machebeuf to remain in Albuquerque. He decided to hold the novena inspite of his feelings. The parishioners finally gave in to Machebeuf and attended confessions held by him. Machebeuf later on informed the populace that he would be moving on to Santa Fe to be closer to his bishop. They now feared that no one would be available to say Mass or dispense the sacraments. Machebeuf assured the parishioners he would return to the Albuquerque parish once a month.

Padre Gallegos, after his suspension, decided to enter into politics. He declared as a candidate for delegate to the United States Congress. His opponent was Dr. William Carr Lane, the former governor of New Mexico. Gallegos ran a hard fought, well organized campaign against Lane and defeated him. The now popular priest won a narrow victory with a margin of 4,971 votes to Lane's 4,526. The padres vote total was a cross-section of the ethnic population with both American and Hispanic New Mexicans going in his favor.

Lamy made plans to go to Rome in January of 1854. He had several objectives to be met on such a trip. He would declare himself as the new bishop of New Mexico at the vatican. Lamy could also recruit priests and attempt to obtain funds for his diocese. He also desired to go to Europe to try to change the boundaries of his diocese now that New Mexico was an Episcopal See. Lamy had been informed of the work of the society of the *Penitentes*, and he then set upon a plan for banishing the group. Padre Martinez pointed out the impropriety of such an action and cautioned Lamy not to make any rash judgements against the brotherhood.

Lamy had purchased a ranch out in the country a few miles from Santa Fe in Tesuque Canyon. He was especially proud of the place and used it as a haven to take him out of the mind pressing problems at Santa Fe. He invited Machebeuf to see it and proudly, calling it his *Villa Pintoresca*, showed him the building, grounds and orchard. Machebeuf was to take over for Lamy during his absence at Rome. Lamy completed his plans and arrangements for the trip. His intention was to take two of the native boys along with

74

him so that they could complete their studies for the priesthood in Europe. One of his students was Eulogio Ortiz, a younger brother of Juan Felipe Ortiz.

Before leaving for Europe, Lamy decided in favor of issuing forth another pastoral letter on January 14, 1854. In the letter he warned everyone that they should learn proper conduct when receiving the sacraments, especially the sacrament of matrimony. He stated, all should pay close attention to their obligation of making payments to the church in order to receive the sacraments. He forewarned that those heads of households that refused to pay the tithes would be penalized in that the rest of the family members would have to pay triple fees. He ordered that

"not a single peso of the holy parish fund was to be spent for theatrical comedies, dances, and other profane diversions," [88]

which many of the Mexican customs seemed to involve.

Lamy also wrote to Archbishop Kenrick to inform him that Padre Gallegos, now that he was New Mexico's delegate at Washington, might try to contact him. Lamy wanted to be certain that Kenrick knew that Gallegos was a suspended priest. If Gallegos would give details of his suspension to the archbishop, he was not to be believed because he had no real proof to support his accusations. Lamy left for Europe, leaving Machebeuf in charge as vicar general.

Gallegos wrote to Bishop Zubiria while in Washington, informing him that,

"His Illustrious Lordship Lamy passed through here on his way to Rome. I assume he is going to justify his behavior before the Holy Father. I am afraid he will discharge upon us the weight of his imputations, so leading the Holy Father to a belief in contradiction of the true facts. The position of my Catholic countrymen is getting worse every day." [89]

Gallegos stated, he was very concerned because a large number of Catholics had "defected to the Protestants."

Lamy wrote to Purcell about his trip to Europe,

"We had a short and good passage. We were on the sea only nine days and one night."

He had sailed from Boston, Massachusetts on March 29, 1854. Arriving in Paris he and his two companions stayed with the Sulpicians in the rue du Bac. Lamy left the two boys to finish their schooling.

Vicar General Machebeuf, back in Albuquerque, had filed a suit against Gallegos for possession of his home which was on Church property. Lamy had once before offered to pay for it. The padre would not leave, but he finally accepted payment from Machebeuf for the home and left.

By June of 1854, Lamy was in Rome. He presented himself as
the new bishop of the Episcopal See of Santa Fe. He was to see
Cardinal Barnabo. Lamy wished to discuss the boundary lines of
his diocese. Before December 30, 1853, the land on the lower
southern area of the territory of New Mexico had belonged to
Mexico. But with the Gadsden Purchase it now belonged to the
United States. Lamy argued that having a Mexican bishop on
American territory could only serve to cause problems for the
United States. There were now many Americans living in that area
and Lamy was afraid that they would refuse to receive the
sacraments from native priests. The Propaganda wrote to Bishop
Zubiria asking for his comments. The bishop in Durango sent a
notarized copy of his original letter of November 1851 to the
Vatican.

Cardinal Barnabo then heard Lamy's version of his problems
with Vicar Juan Felipe Ortiz. Barbabo wrote to the Bishop of
Durango and asked him to correct the situation with Ortiz to
Lamy's satisfaction. Lamy purchased paintings and other items for
his churches while in Rome. He was also able to convince a Father
Damaso Taladrid to return with him to New Mexico. Lamy was,
through diplomatic channels, able to obtain an audience with the
Pope. He informed Pius IX about the flagellant brotherhood of
Penitentes in his diocese.

"The Pope made it clear that the bishop should try to disband
the order..." [90]

The Pope presented Lamy with a chalice out of the papal treasury.
After his audience with Pio Nono, Lamy was able to leave in the
direction of Clermont. There he was able to recruit three priests,
Pierre Eguillon, N. Juilliard, and Antoine Avel; Jean Guerin, a
deacon; Eugene Pollet and Sebastien Vaur, subdeacons, and two
laymen, Vaur and Rimbert. They were to be trained by Lamy in
Santa Fe.

From Clermont Lamy went to Lempdes on a visit to his brother.
Before leaving he was able to obtain a loan from him of twenty-five
thousand francs. He also appealed to the Society for the
Propaganda of the Faith in Lyon for more priests. He reported to
the society about the people's lack of religion in New Mexico. This,
he added, was the blame of the incapable native clergy. Conditions
in New Mexico were horrible and the Society, even with Lamy's
descriptive detail, could not even imagine it. They were also able
to give him twenty thousand more francs to use in his work in
New Mexico.

Lamy and his group set sail from Le Havre to America on August
1, 1854. After twelve days on the open sea they arrived in New

York. On November 18, 1854, they arrived in Santa Fe. Vicar Machebeuf assigned Father Juilliard to Belen, Father Martin to Isleta, south of Albuquerque, and Father Avel to Santa Fe.

Upon Lamy's return he again received a letter from Padre Martinez. The padre accused Machebeuf of suspending several priests while Lamy was in Rome. According to Martinez the Vicar General had taken the benefices of the suspended priests and pastors. Padre Martinez sent notarized written testimony of witnesses against Machebeuf to Lamy. He went on to denounce Machebeuf for his actions against Padre Gallegos of Albuquerque.

Martinez had received authority from Bishop Zubiria to administer the Sacrament of Confirmation, which was usually reserved to bishops. Zubiria had been empowered by Pope Gregory XVI to delegate the authority to the most influential priests within the span of his jurisdictional area. Padre Martinez was selected for the northern territory of New Mexico, and he was granted extensive powers. [91] The padre informed Lamy that he had continued exercising his authority and confirmed during the bishop's many absences from New Mexico.

Padre Martinez at one time had told Lamy that he had been given a delegation by the next-to-the-last active custodian (Franciscan) of New Mexico. It was approved by Bishop Zubiria in 1833. He could receive the faithful in novitiate and give them the protection of the Third Order of St. Francis of Assisi in the Order of Penance. He could also apply to them sung Masses (say Mass for them) in the Church of St. Francis of Ranchos de Taos on the 4th Sunday of each month.

On the bishop's return from Rome, he told the priest that he had expressed authority from the Pope to eradicate the penitente brotherhood. The priest then acknowledged, he would be forced to comply with such an order and would abide by it. The members of the society of Jesus of Nazareth were then threatened with excommunication if

"certain abuses practiced by the members in the name of religion were continued."

Confident of a victory, the bishop again turned his attention to the opposition of his tithing and another problem that annoyed him.

The churches and chapels of the Diocese were filled with "primitive statues and paintings on wood." Lamy recalled reading of the "distasteful images" in the reports. One such report described them as ludicrous, grotesque, laughable and comical. Concerning the representation of St. Michael, the patron saint of San Miguel del Bado, the writer stated,

"A more comical figure than this same San Miguel it would be difficult either to imagine or discover. I cannot say that his

77

saintship had ever been tarred, but he had certainly been feathered from head to foot. From his shoulders hung listlessly a pair of hugh, illconstructed wings, while his head to complete the ludicrous *tout ensemble*, was covered with a lace cap of the fashion of our grandmothers...Nothing could be more grotesque and laughable than this comical head of St. Michael,...'' [92]

Now on seeing them firsthand, Lamy could not beyond his wildest imagination, see how the priests had allowed them to grace the churches. Lamy's disapproval of the New Mexican santero folk art was so marked that he circulated a mandate that they be removed from all of the churches and chapels of the territory and replaced with conventional plaster images, prints, and paintings on canvas. [93] This was met with complete disbelief on the part of the people and they rejected the thought of losing their sacred images. They were *Santos* that they and their families had created and prayed to, in envisioning Christ and the saints. Now they regarded them as a part of the family and just as essential in their daily lives as eating and sleeping. Lamy's order was met with indignation.

On March of 1855, Lamy sent Machebeuf off on a journey. He was to return to New Mexico with four Loretto nuns from St. Louis. As it were, it was an opportune time for Machebeuf to head East. After spending some time in Kentucky he and the nuns left for Kansas on June 7th.

In the meantime, Vicar Ortiz returned to Santa Fe from Durango. He had a grave fever on his return trip. On his arrival in Santa Fe he found out that Lamy was on a pastoral visit to southern New Mexico. Padre Jose Ortiz was called away to church affairs in another parish. He asked the vicar to take his place in the services of the feast day of San Juan held on June 19 in Santa Fe. Vicar Ortiz graciously consented. Lamy returned to the capital city from his pastoral visit. Vicar Juan Felipe Ortiz, after hearing that Lamy was back in Santa Fe, went to see him. Lamy then suspended him for having taken Padre Jose Ortiz' place on the feast day without his permission. Vicar Ortiz wrote an explanation as to why he had felt compelled to serve on the feast day.

Lamy sent word to Ortiz that he wished to see him. The vicar asked Lamy for his old Santa Fe parish. Lamy's answer was that he could no longer have the parish, but that he could be sent to Pena Blanca instead. Ortiz maintained that he was the ''irremovable pastor'' of St. Francis and furthermore, did not want any other parish. Lamy would no longer speak to the vicar. Ortiz gathered some of his personal belongings and left.

Lamy accused Ortiz of taking church property. The municipal

prefect at Santa Fe made a ruling that the objects did indeed belong to the vicar. Lamy wrote to the Vatican,

"as the authorities are on his side, and I must say are rather scandalous Catholics, we have to suffer these abuses. I am telling you these facts so that if you receive in Rome some documents on the subject, you will have already been informed..."[94]

On July 16, Machebeuf and the nuns were crossing the plains of Kansas with a trading caravan to New Mexico. On July 24, 1855, they arrived at Santa Fe. The group was joyously received by Lamy.

Vicar Ortiz wrote a letter to Bishop Zubiria, outlining his discoveries at Santa Fe. Several items which had been donated to the church by his relatives and himself including: chalices, a censer, a pyx and a silver box were taken to Europe by Lamy. For what purpose it was not known. He also stated,

"many of the cathedral vestments had been burned, along with forty different costumes once used to dress the statue of Our Lady of the Rosary [La Conquistadora]"[95]

These had been laboriously woven and embroidered by the faithful of New Mexico. Also the division of the Santa Fe parish was highly questionable. La Castrense, which was to have been restored, was now in a delapidated state. Furthermore, Lamy was using the St. Francis church as his cathedral. Lamy wrote to Purcell,

"Some of our Mexican padres are more troublesome to us than the 'know-nothings' with you."[96]

Lamy was very angry about the turn of events with Ortiz. It annoyed him that the people should take such a stance against his wishes. He went as far as to invoke the help of an alcalde's court to secure collection of his tithes. He began to threaten excommunication against anyone not following his mandates. The bishop sent out another pastoral letter. He informed the people that they would be celebrating the Feast of the Immaculate Conception in December (the people in New Mexico had always held a novena for the Blessed Virgin Mary in December) as would be the entire Catholic World. Pius IX had declared the Dogma of the Immaculate Conception the year before. Lamy instructed that everyone should receive the sacraments in honor of Our Lady.

Lamy sternly announced that

"Any family which does not fulfill the fifth precept of the Church, will not have the right to receive the Holy Sacraments. Let us again inform you that we consider these as not belonging to the Church who do not observe this precept; and we likewise would take away all faculties to say Mass and administer the sacraments from all Pastors who failed to sustain and provide for the maintenance of religion and its ministers, in proportion to the goods which God has given them."[97]

By January 28, 1856, Padre Martinez sent his cousin, Joaquin Sandoval, to deliver a letter and a silver chalice to Lamy. He stated, he was unable to go himself because he was suffering from rheumatism which caused much pain in his legs when riding. Often he was unable to sleep till three in the morning because of illness. He felt, if he did not get well he might have to resign but until then he would continue with all of his duties. But if there was anything he could do, he would be very happy to help. Lamy never answered his letter. He felt, he had more important matters to attend to.

The tithing fees were for the most part excessive with no allowances for the poor. Yet, Lamy claimed that the former "fees were enormous."

"If they must bury the dead, each internment cost sixteen piasters ($16.00). In the pathetic values of most families such fees in the aggregate of a lifetime's pious needs amounted to a fortune."[98]

As an example, Lamy's fee for a burial amounted to a total of $141.00 (these were the bishop's REDUCED fees).

"In the spring of 1856, a young Mexican gentlemen was buried in Santa Fe according to the rites of the Catholic Church...the bill...presented for the services..."

was:

"Dobles (tolling of the bells)	$ 10.00
El sepulcro (the grave)	30.00
La cruz alta (the grand cross)	1.00
La capa (high mass vestments)	3.00
La agua bendita (the holy water)	1.00
Los ciriales (candlesticks)	1.00
El incensario (the incense holder)	1.00
La mesa (resting place)	3.00
El entierro (the interment)	30.00
La misa (the mass)	20.00
El organo (the organ)	15.00
Los cantores (the singers of the mass)	6.00
El responso del oratorio (response of the oratorio)	10.00
Mas al diacono (the deacons fee, additional)	10.00
	$141.00 [99]

William Watts Hart Davis, United States Attorney to the territory of New Mexico wrote of the burial fees,

80

"It must be borne in mind that these charges are solely the dues of the Church for the religious services of the burial, and the bills are made out in mercantile form and duly presented for payment. From this showing, it is an expensive matter to die and be buried in New Mexico, and appears to cost quite as much as it does to live. There is no doubt about the right of the Church to charge for the burial service, all the people are willing to pay, but we may fairly question the propriety of making such simple and necessary rites so expensive...Facts of this kind are a strong argument in favor of the abolition of the system of tithing in New Mexico. Religion and the attending rites should not be made a luxury only to be enjoyed by the rich, but all its offices and consolations should be within the reach of the poorest in the land." [100]

Concerning the tithes in New Mexico, the U.S. Attorney continued,

"Another abuse that should be remedied is the high price of marriage, baptismal, and burial fees that the Church exacts from the people. In the case of marriage the high rates have heretofore prevented lawful wedlock, and driven a large portion of the population into licentiousness. They were not able to pay the fees demanded by the priest, and no civil officer had power to unite people in matrimony...

"The regular fees for marriage and burial service have in some instances been known to be as high as four and five hundred dollars, the price always being regulated by the length and kind of ceremony, and, in the case of burial, by the number of masses said for the repose of the soul. It sometimes costs the poor peasant the greater part of his worldly store to have his children baptized. This ceremony becomes a matter of great solicitude with the mother, since those who are not baptized are supposed to dwell in Limbo when they die, while those who receive this rite of the Church are placed in the regions of eternal happiness." [101]

Many of the people were unable to pay for their religious services and began to suffer undue hardships. On one occasion Lamy charged close to $1,600 for the funeral of Gertrudis Barcelo Among the items included for her funeral were:

"*los derechos del obispo* (the rights of the bishop,) one thousand dollars; *los pasos*, fifty dollars, which means that each time the procession halted on its way to the burial and the bier was placed upon the ground, the Church made a charge of this amount; and the other charges were in proportion." [102]

Lamy was aware of a petition that was being readied by the

citizens and native priests of New Mexico which was to be directed to the Pope. In January of 1856, he wrote to Barnabo,

"Perhaps the legislators of New Mexico who, though Catholics in name, are far from honoring religion by their moral conduct, will send you a representation against me and some of the rules which I established. I think it my duty to warn you of this, for all this opposition is plotted slyly by two or three Mexican priests who do not easily pardon me for the fault of having come to trouble them..." [103]

Both Lamy and Machebeuf worked at developing a lengthy defense against the charges. Their defense was based upon the derision of all the priests and citizens whose names might appear on the petition. Degrading statements were aimed at making the accusations appear limp and unsubstantiated. Lamy once again asked for his diocese to include Donana which until now still belonged to Zubiria. He again repeated his reasons from his last trip to Rome.

In February, Lamy wrote to Barnabo,

"the inhabitants of the Condado are astonished that I do not exercise my jurisdiction in this part of the Territory as in the other parts...several bishops and archbishops of the United States" would unite with him "to demonstrate to the Holy See the justice" of his petition for the area. "M. Machebeuf will expose to you the various reasons why the Holy See should deign to grant my request, for the order and general well-being of our holy religion." [104]

Lamy also asked if it would be possible for him to sell *La Castrense* since he needed more funds and it was no longer being used.

By March of 1856, Machebeuf had already left Santa Fe for his journey to Europe. He would reach Clermont by the end of May.

Rev. Philbert Martin had been assigned by Machebeuf to the Isleta Pueblo, south of Albuquerque, on November of 1854 where he remained until 1856. During this time Dolores Perea of Isleta informed Bishop Lamy,

"of the scandals Father Martin is causing by having a woman of bad fame in the community as his housekeeper."

Father Martin was removed from Isleta and transferred to another parish.

Lamy wrote to Purcell in April of 1856,

"...where I have good priests, the improvement is sensible... The priests I brought two years ago, and to whom you yourself gave hospitality in Cincinnati are doing great good. they are animated of the right kind of spirit. I hope Mr. Machebeuf will bring me a few more of that kind..." [105]

Lamy at another time added,

"Though the time rolls on, the strong opposition raised altogether by few of the old padres does not seem to stop." [106]

Gallegos was once again campaigning for reelection as delegate to the Congress. Lamy supported his opponent, Miguel A. Otero, and on occasion spoke on his behalf. Both Otero and Gallegos were gearing for strong campaigns. It would appear that the election would involve Lamy forces against the native forces. Concerning the campaign Lamy said, they are

"trying all they can to embarrass us." [107]

In a letter dated April 22, 1856, Padre Martinez requested that a native priest be appointed as his assistant in Taos. He could therefore be prepared for a smooth transition into the position of pastor upon his retirement. The priest felt, Padre Ramon Medina was the logical person for his replacement because he knew the people and area well. He cautioned Lamy that the parishioners would resent the placement of a priest other than a native. Padre Martinez mentioned, the parishioners did not believe in the *Americanos*. He had tried fruitlessly to change their minds. Once he had trained his substitute and the new priest was ready to continue alone he would "formally resign."

A petition along with substantiating documents was addressed to Pope Pius IX. It was signed by thirty of the thirty-nine members of the two Houses of the Territorial Legislature. The petition was delivered by Vicar Juan Felipe Ortiz in Rome. Vicar Ortiz was apparently notified of his possible elevation to the higher position in the Episcopal See of Santa Fe. Upon arrival at the Vatican in Rome he presented himself as the Bishop of New Mexico. Lamy was promptly informed, possibly by Barnabo. Lamy wrote, Vicar Ortiz

"had the humility to propose himself to Rome as Bishop of the Diocese and to have us suspended or at least removed." [108]

Vicar Juan Felipe Ortiz wrote to Lamy asking him to prove by document that he was, in reality, the one empowered to assume the position. Lamy's response,

"this very week he wrote me an isolent letter, asking me to show him a Document of the Sovereign Pontife [sic] by which I could prove that I was authorized to take this parish." [109]

Lamy was very much exasperated with the questioning of his authority for he added,

"From these facts you may have an idea of their ability." [111]

A gross error had apparently been made in the higher echelons of the Vatican. But whatever the case, there was an appeal from those petitioning the Pope that the

"Most Holy Father, with all such remarkable facts, and they

are so of a certainty, for causes so serious and grave and just, we do beg Your Holiness, and we pray in the most humble and respectful way, that You deign to decree for us, according to our petition, the removal from his place as Bishop of Santa Fe, His Illustrious Lordship Lamy; and the nomination in his place of the Vicar Don Juan Felipe Ortiz, in which individual, we have no doubt in telling Your Holiness, that those qualities stipulated by Saint Paul as necessary for the exact fulfillment of the heavy episcopal responsibilities, are found...Such a substitution will return the peace and tranquility to our Church, and will preserve us firm and stable in our true Catholicism, producing at the same time great joy and happiness for the majority of the Faithful of this Bishopric." [112]

The formal petition to the Pope dated April 24, 1856 read in part:

"Most Holy Father: I have the honor of presenting to the special consideration of Your Holiness the attached pages which were consigned to me by my constituents of the Territory of New Mexico.

"The complaint which they contain against His Illustrious Lordship Lamy is true, just, and honest; for which reason I believe they will merit the worthy attention of Your Holiness; so that by estimating the deeds in their just merits, Your Holiness may then resolve them in the most understanding and appropriate manner.

"With all my soul I regret to find myself the one to reveal such sad truths, which should always be hidden in the pages of history. But their revelation has become necessary, since the spiritual and temporal welfare of the Catholic Faithful of New Mexico depends upon it.

"The conduct, Most Holy Father, the unfriendly conduct of his Illustrious Lordship Senor Lamy without just cause and without observance of the necessary rules as demanded by Canon Law, has deprived the permanent pastors of the Church of New Mexico of their proper benefices, while substituting in their places other ministers newly emigrated to this country, whom he has favored, conferring on them many benefices, thus leaving our poor previous ministers without their posts of spiritual administrations, and forcing them into the hard position of having to work in menial and crude task, in order to make a living.

"Our Christian Pueblos of Indians, numbering some eighteen pueblos, are thus also left without spiritual administration, harshly abandoned to their own ignorance; and I have no doubt that within a short time they will revert to their primitive and savage state of idolatry...

"I have been informed that no sooner was Senor Lamy notified of the accusations thus made than he immediately ordered the Vicar P. Machebeuf to hurry to Rome...to try to mislead with false information, which we hope Your Holiness will not believe, and will consequently take needed action on such an important matter...

"Your most loving son, who humbly asks Your Blessing, and who attentively, Kisses Your Hands, J.M. Gallegos, Delegate of New Mexico in the Congress of the Union."

In substantiating documents there was included: Lamy's illegal division of the Parish of Santa Fe and ultimate removal of it from the jurisdiction of Vicar Juan Felipe Ortiz; the suspension of native priests without canonical warnings and against the wishes of the parishioners; he had ignored petitions sent to him asking for him to amend his abuses of church law in regard to the suspensions; Machebeuf's loose and scandalous activities at Pena Blanca and Albuquerque; Lamy's imposition of enormous tithes and heavy penalties for non-payment; Lamy had condoned Machebeuf's offensive characterization of certain marriages. Lamy, contrary to public statutes, had taken part in and interfered with New Mexico's political affairs by campaigning for a candidate to the U.S. Congress. It was further added that the people, in their resentment against Lamy and his vicar, were defecting to the Protestants. [113]

In a letter to the editor of the Santa Fe Weekly Gazette, J. L. Collins, dated Saturday, May 4, 1856, Padre Martinez informed the people of New Mexico of his desire to resign his position as pastor at Taos. He listed as his reasons for his intended resignation: his age, illnesses, loss of strength and endurance to do all of the work required, including taking care of and repairing the church and its roofs plus the cemetery. Mentioning as his main reason for his thought of resigning was his objection to Lamy's Pastoral letter of January 14, 1854, in which he ordered, the priests were to

"exclude from the sacraments all household heads who refused to pay the tithes, and to demand triple fees for Baptisms from other members of such families."

Priests not complying with his order were subject to strong penalty. The padre felt that in all clear conscience he could not comply with such an order. Feeling that it was unjust, he felt that he should resign rather than carry it out. He promised he would submit a formal resignation if and when a native priest had been sent to replace him, and he had properly trained him to assume the duties of the parish. [114]

Lamy, taking advantage of the situation, accepted a resignation which Martinez had not submitted. The bishop sent Damaso Taladrid to take up the position. Writing to the priest on May 5, he stated, he would send Taladrid in place of Medina "who is still far behind" so that he could now settle back and relax in the advanced age in which "he [Martinez] finds himself."[115]

Martinez was filled with disbelieving shock when Taladrid arrived to release the priest of his duties. Padre Martinez did not know of Lamy's feelings toward him and thought the bishop was just considering his health. Padre Martinez allowed Taladrid to remain as long as he could continue to say Mass and dispense the sacraments. Bishop Lamy had brought Taladrid to New Mexico along with several Frenchmen to replace some of the native priests. Taladrid became Lamy's confidant. The bishop felt that Taladrid would be a perfect replacement and match for Martinez. Padre Martinez informed Bishop Lamy, he had not released his delegation of the Third Order of St. Francis of Assisi in the Order of Penance to Taladrid. It was a personal delegation and not as priest of Taos. He asked for the bishop's decision on this matter. There was no reply.

The people steadfastly refused to accept Taladrid as a replacement for their priest. They began a movement against him soon after his arrival. Padre Martinez finally pacified the situation by telling them, he was still the *Parochus Propruis* (Pastor) of Taos. He would not relinquish his title to Taladrid but would turn over some of the administration to him.

Pius IX had already received the petition and substantiating documents sent by the legislative assembly when Machebeuf arrived at the Vatican in June. The Pope asked the office of the Propaganda Fide to investigate the charges made against Lamy. The charges were presented to Machebeuf.

Machebeuf issued a rebuttal of the charges brought against him and Lamy by the people of New Mexico saying,

"It is necessary to observe that the inhabitants of New Mexico are generally deprived of all schooling and are little accustomed to governing themselves according to the law of the United States. The immense majority do not know how to read and those who are able to sign their name are considered educated..."[116]

He described the legislative assembly as

"composed of ignorant men, most of them corrupt, dishonest, who hold the people in fear of them,...and the corruption of this society illustrates their prejudice toward a foreign bishop who is obliged to reform their morals..."[117]

Machebeuf's main defense was that the people of New Mexico

were illiterate. Machebeuf then gave slandering descriptions of the lives of the "ignorant, dishonest, and corrupt men" who were making the accusations. Such men as, "Fathers J.F. Ortiz, Salazar, Lujan, Gallegos, and Martinez.[118] He did say of Padre Martinez, "he has never failed in a show of personal respect towards Bishop Lamy."

Lamy had already written to Barnabo twice, before Machebeuf's arrival in Rome warning him of what to expect from the legislator's. He felt it best Barnabo should be ready for them. From the time that Barnabo had become Prefect of the Sacred Congregation of the Propaganda Fide in Rome, Lamy had asked,

"if I must depend on your protection, I ask that it be available to me..."[119]

Barnabo now made a summary of Machebeuf's report before presenting it to the Pope.

Archbishop Clementi in Mexico City wrote to the Vatican asking that a decision on the disputed boundaries be made. He sent another copy of Zubiria's original letter of 1851 showing Zubiria'a and Lamy's mutual agreement concerning the boundaries. Lamy had continued sending letters to Zubiria requesting that the bishop give him Donana. Machebeuf gave the same reasons Lamy had given before as to the placement of the county in his diocese. The

Pope had not made a decision on the matters when Machebeuf left in August.

Taladrid in New Mexico, who already considered himself the pastor of Taos, viewed Padre Martinez with contempt. He sought every means to discredit the priest and elevate his own position in the eyes of the bishop and people. Taladrid wrote to Lamy,

"The only human thing about him is his shape."

He made it more and more difficult for the aged and sick priest to say Mass, even going as far as willfully inflicting suffering on him.

Padre Martinez would enjoy saying Mass in the church early in the mornings. Taladrid, however, made this difficult. Taladrid was quite aware that the old padre could not sustain a long fast before Mass due to his ill health. He consequently instructed the sexton to delay the preparation of the vestments and holy vessels so that Martinez would be forced to wait.[120] In May of 1856, Padre Martinez finally went to Taladrid's home to appeal to him. He pleaded with Taladrid to restrain his vengefulness and allow him to continue saying Mass without the hardships he was placing on him. Taladrid grabbed Martinez' hands violently and told the much older priest that he knew how to fight and fight hard. Taladrid went on to say, the bishop held him in very bad regard and he would always have Martinez "in reprobation." Padre Martinez had never shown anything but "personal respect toward the bishop."[121] He could not believe what Taladrid had said. But Taladrid continued. He began to strike out at his family. In one instance he treated "a Martinez cousin 'as a heretic'."[122] Padre Martinez, finally placed beyond all endurance, began to say Mass at a private chapel.

The campaign for New Mexico's delegate to Congress continued. Bishop Lamy and Miguel A. Otero were apparently of one mind. Their feelings about the Church and the people of New Mexico were similar. The *Weekly Gazette* of Santa Fe endorsed Otero? An editorial against Gallegos read:

"We ask the people of New Mexico in the name of all that's just, to look at the acts of Bishop Lamy since he came into the territory. Has he done anything that is not calculated to elevate the Church, and to advance the interests of the Holy Catholic religion? Has he not relieved the people from oppressive Church exactions levied solely to maintain a corrupt and profligate Clergy, who were in may cases a moral curse to the country? Pause, Mexicans, before you cast your votes for a man who would stop the progress of this glorious reform, in which you are so much interested for yourselves and your children in all time to come."[123]

Gallegos was reelected. Otero went before the Congress to

contest the election of Gallegos. Gallegos had won by a majority of 578 votes, 131 ballots being from Donana. Lamy in 1854 while in Rome had stated,

"the inhabitants always voted in the New Mexico civil elections,"

when he had requested that Donana be put in his diocese. Otero claimed, Gallegos could not represent all the people of New Mexico. He had sought out the Mexican vote and campaigned against the American party. Otero had been educated in Lamy's school, his family was well-to-do and could speak English. The ballots from Donana were rejected because Otero argued, the area was comprised mainly of Mexican residents. Lamy felt this was to his advantage. This gave him a case to present to Rome as to why Donana should be part of his diocese. He had written to Rome and was waiting for their reply.

Gallegos in Washington stated,

"A clergyman of that church [Catholic], I found myself, previous to my first election to this body, deprived of my living in common with all the other native clergy of New Mexico, excepting four only, by the new French bishop, to make way for imported French priest of his own selection. The attempt to vindicate our rights only served to secure the whole weight of ecclesiastical influence against us, one and all. At the second election, now the subject of contest, it is notorious that the foreign bishop did, in fact, intermeddle, by himself and his priests, not to support me, but to crush me, and to secure the election of my opponent." [124]

The first part of the debate had concerned the acceptance of the Donana ballots. Otero now turned to the vindication of Lamy. One part of Otero's defense stated,

"...at the time of the acquisition of New Mexico by this country, when the new bishop was sent out, he found the Church sunk into the most deplorable condition of immorality. The priests themselves were notoriously addicted to the grossest vices. They were, in many instances, the disgrace of every gambling house and drinking saloon, and the open frequenters of brothels. In a word, they personified vice in all its hideous and revolting aspects (echoes of Machebeuf in Rome). The good bishop, seeing how the holy office had been prostituted and the Church disgraced, proceeded at once to remove the delinquent priests, and substituted others in their stead. This is what the bishop has done: 'this is the head and front of his offending'." [125]

The elected delegate from New Mexico was removed from office and Otero put in his place.

In August, Machebeuf was headed back for New Mexico bringing with him six seminarians: J. M. Coudert, Gabriel Ussel, Fialon, Fayst, Ralliere, Truchard and from St. Louis, Thomas Hayes.

Taladrid continued to "defame" Padre Martinez. The priest wrote asking Lamy, if Taladrid was doing this with his knowledge and approval. He also informed the bishop that Taladrid was gathering some defenders for himself. Also that Taladrid had replaced the

"church vessels of silver with others of tin."[126]

Again there was no reply from Lamy. Martinez felt there was no recourse but to write an attack upon the administration of the Catholic Church in New Mexico which was published in the Santa Fe Weekly *Gazette* of September 3, 1856.

Lamy found an opportunity to counter with a drastic punishment. In a letter dated September 19, 1856, the bishop suspended all of Martinez' powers to act as a priest at Arroyo Hondo, which was under Martinez' jurisdiction as Pastor at Taos. He also suspended his rights to say Mass and administer the sacraments in the Bishopric, unless he should issue a retraction of his article. The priest, in a lengthy defense, pointed out the impropriety of Lamy's action. He would not comply with it being that the bishop's act was not sanctioned by official church law. [127]

According to Martinez, Lamy had not allowed for due process, no opportunity was given him to make a defense before a tribunal convened for the purpose of suspension. The bishop did not state specific reasons required by law for suspension, and as far as the article in the Gazette was concerned, it was his right to state his opinion on any subject as an American citizen as stated in the Bill of Rights. He brought to Lamy's attention decrees of Canon law and sent him two volumes on *Leyes Canonicas* (Canon Law) to study at his leisure.

Martinez later wrote that his statements in the *Gazette* went further than intended, but his opinion was still in the light of justice. He complained about his undefined suspension and affirmed that he would give the bishop every recognition as long as he stayed within the boundaries of canon law.

Padre Taladrid began to approach the Penitentes with promises of their acceptance and protection by the bishop if they would allow him (Taladrid) to reorganize their Brotherhood. Word reached Martinez of Taladrid's promises to the Brothers. He again wrote to the bishop for an explanation of Taladrid's sudden involvement with the Brotherhood. Padre Martinez reminded Bishop Lamy, while on his last trip to Santa Fe, His Grace had expressly stated, he had an order from the Pope to eliminate the

Penitente Brotherhood.

On October 25, 1856, Martinez wrote another article to the Santa Fe *Gazette* enumerating the reasons why he believed the tithing should be removed in New Mexico. He also felt, it was his right as an American citizen to express himself freely concerning anything that involved the citizens of the nation. He believed any American citizen should be able to do this without the threat of being censored whether by the government or by church officials.

The priest continued saying Mass and dispensing the sacraments at several other chapels including the *moradas*. These included those of the Duran family chapel at Talpa, that of Ranchos de Taos, Rio Chiquito (now Talpa), and the Carmen Oratory at Llano de Talpa, among others. Several of these had been dedicated to Padre Martinez' personal use.[128]

There are many private chapels throughout the territory of New Mexico. Several had been built in the early years of Spanish colonization to provide a place of worship for outlying settlements. The residents of the larger communities had the comforts of a parish church within easy access. The people of the isolated villages had to travel over large distances to attend Mass or receive the sacraments. Padre Martinez, as well as other pastors, saw the need for more churches in the territory. The priests appealed to the people and the wealthier citizens erected private chapels dedicated to the saints and placed at the disposal of the resident pastors of the nearest towns.

The chapels were later blessed and consecreated by Bishop Zubiria during his visitations. They also housed countless carved and painted religious images, *santos* and *retablos*, made by local *santeros*. When a community resident felt the need to pray he went to the chapel which was open to all, day and night. Prayer meetings were held daily and not a single Holy Day went by without being observed at the chapels.

When the bishop learned that there were no tithes being sent from these chapels he requested papers on all the private chapels of the area.

On November 10, 1856, Machebeuf arrived in Santa Fe. The Vicar General, brought some good news to Lamy from Barnabo. Barnabo was in full agreement with Lamy about charges that had been brought against him. He also gave Lamy permission to see *La Castrense*. The six seminarians who had come with Machebeuf were ordained a month later at the Loretto convent. They did not know how to speak Spanish or English and were nervous about their assignments. Gabriel Ussel was sent to Arroyo Hondo to replace Lucero. Coudert was assigned as Machebeuf's assistant in Albuquerque.

By December, 1856, the bishop was faced with yet another problem. Two factions were developing among the people of Belen. One wishing the old church rebuilt and the other following the lead of their new pastor, Father Eugenio Paulet, and the Bishop, desiring a new church. The Bishop declared that

"all who persist in their intention of rebuilding the old church, or of retaining the sacred vessels, statues, etc., shall be excommunicated, and any priest who should say Mass in the old church will be suspended." [129]

Things began to settle down a little after many had been excommunicated. Bishop Lamy, in a letter to Father Paulet gave him full faculties to absolve

"all from excommunication who shall retract before witnesses." [130]

In February of 1857 in another letter he forbade Father Paulet to

"administer any sacraments to those who refuse such retraction before witnesses." [131]

In January 1857, Lamy wrote to Barnabo thanking him for his help in his defense against the petition sent to the Vatican. He also asked Barnabo why Donana was still not assigned to him. Lamy could no longer argue that Zubiria was neglecting the people of that area. The bishop of Durango assigned the area to Ramon Ortiz as Vicar Forane (rural dean). Lamy sent Barnabo copies of both Gallegos' and Otero's debates. Lamy argued, having Donana under Zubiria had caused a problem in the voting procedure. By February 1857, Lamy had not yet received an answer on the disputed area. He again wrote to Barnabo using the same argument.

Bishop Lamy sent Machebeuf on a trip to Mississippi. On the way there some Indians went into Machebeuf's camp. They were hungry. Machebeuf gave one of them a spoonful of pepper and said the Indian had given

"a free exhibition of facial contortion which was interesting and amusing...to another he gave a spoonful of vinegar and the Indian began to cough.. " [132]

When writing of the account, Machebeuf said he later offered the Indians coffee, sugar and biscuits. On his return trip, Lamy's niece, Marie, a friend of hers, a French gardener, three Mexican servants, one Irish seminarian and twelve others accompanied Machebeuf from Mississippi to Santa Fe.

In March of 1857, Lamy wrote to Purcell

"the opposition we met at our first coming here, and which manifested itself on several occasions, is far from being crushed down. Their number, we hope, are diminishing, but unfortunately, the less they seem to be, the more head strong

92

they are getting. The few native clergy that are out of their office keep up a bad spirit against us..."[133]

In a long letter to the bishop on April 13, 1857, Padre Martinez took issue with two provisions of his Pastoral letter of 1854. One of the provisions concerned the living of couples in proper matrimony:

"Those living in sin [without being properly married] are scandalous to the faithful."

The priest mentioned, information he had received against the bishop's premise disturbed him greatly. He had been informed,

"through an order of the bishop, Padre Rafael Chavez in Sebolleta [sic] married Francisco Sandabas to Maria Clara Sanchez, who was already married to one Antonio Padilla. Also, in Pecos, Vicar Machebeuf married Joaquin Lopez to one woman and Lopez was later remarried in Santa Fe to Maria Guadalupe Sena."

Martinez stated,

"There are many other cases in which individuals already married were remarried with others." [134]

This seemed to him completely contrary to the bishop's rule on matrimony. He felt, the bigamous state of the couples went against the teachings of Christ.

Mentioning rule five on tithing, he stated, the United States government did not sanction enforced collection of tithing or compelled a citizen to pay it [in reference to the bishop's use of the courts].

In the same letter Martinez also declared, his objections to Taladrid were based upon his desire to have his parish administered by a priest with good qualities for the spiritual needs and welfare of his people. He requested that Taladrid be recalled and another priest sent in his place. [135]

Taladrid continued attacking Padre Martinez. Rather than orally, he was now doing it in print in articles sent to the Gaceta. Now that there was proof in writing of Taladrid's behavior Lamy could no longer ignore it. Bishop Lamy was having problems at the same time with another one of his French priests, Father Martin, assigned to Isleta. He was being charged with bad moral conduct which was causing scandal in the pueblo. Lamy decided to remove Martin and replace him with Taladrid. Taladrid would be replaced at Taos by Father Eulogio Ortiz. The bishop now made plans for Padre Martinez' excommunication.

In a letter to Machebeuf dated May 2, 1857, Padre Martinez referred to the

"conversation about the issues...you had with me the evening of the 19th of April"

93

in Taos. In reference to Bishop Lamy, Martinez wrote in his defense:

"...not complying with canon law, he wants to proceed against me...in not complying, the result is disobedience to the laws of the Church, in which he is bound to follow official procedures, and in not doing so,"

makes his action, "nullified." He assures the vicar,

"the rights that I have in canon laws and in our liberal Republican government, in all I have confidence."[136]

He continued,

"The principle issue at hand is the contents of the Pastoral letter of January 14, 1854 for the 5th rule and also the 2nd."

Martinez felt he could not retract his article in the *Gazette* against the letter

"because of the damage that it is causing to the Catholic people of New Mexico...and because of this he [the bishop] should not feel offended..."

The padre said,

"the people would not readily understand this precept."

He referred to the Gospel of St. Matthew, Chapter 23 of putting an

"end to secular revenues of the clergy, wanting to bring to an end the payment of tithes, first fruits, rates for sacraments, free offerings, and various other grants to the Church,"

which he felt were made with "much clarity." He went on to say,

"It can thus be seen and to prove it: some of the confessions that are asked for by those that are sick always commence with being asked if their tithes have been paid, if they have money and what other interests they have..."[137]

The threat of harsher penalties to be inflicted upon the priest, brought him to mention,

"The boisterous noise that has been caused in the vicinity these day, even to saying that the civil authorities, armed forces of the same inhabitants, and even the troops of the government will be sent against me, which none are under your disposal, gives more explanation as to the intention that motivates you [and Lamy] against the priests of the country [natives] that try to retain their rights, and also against the same faithful inhabitants of New Mexico, while the exaction of monies and interests are called apparently, 'Catholic Faith,' as Taladrid asserts in his famous libel which appeared in the *Gazette* of Santa Fe "[138]

With the arrival of Ortiz, Padre Martinez declared himself overjoyed with the solution and most grateful to the bishop.[139] Eulogio Ortiz, the brother of Vicar Ortiz, had gone to Rome with Lamy in 1854. On his return to New Mexico in 1857, Lamy ordained him. He was then assigned to Taos. Martinez, however, still asserted, he was the *Parochus Proprius* of Taos (irremovable rector), he had not as yet formally resigned, and viewed Ortiz as an assistant whom he would train and hand over administrative duties to gradually.

In June 1857, Machebeuf arrived in Taos to commence the oral excommunication of Martinez. He then went on to Arroyo Hondo to excommunicate another native priest that opposed Lamy's policies, Padre Mariano de Jesus Lucero. Martinez nor Lucero made a public response to Machebeuf. The people were loyal to Martinez and angered by the bishop's actions. The padre cautioned, they should always respect the ministers of the church. On Machebeuf's final return to Taos the parishioners returned to their homes in silence. Machebeuf on leaving to Santa Fe with his assistant, Ussel, apparently felt remorse for he commented,

> "It is always the way. Bishop Lamy is sure to send me when there is a bad case to be settled; I am always the one to whip the cats."[140]

Padre Martinez again viewed the sanctions as illegal because they were not based on Canon law. In a letter to Lamy he wrote,

> "It is my right to say: that a bishop cannot remove a pastor from his *parochus proprius* which has been delegated to him by an Ecclesiastical Synod; in my case it is being attempted without a formal judicial trial, against the laws of the church. The well known author of Canon law, Murillo, states in volume 5, decree number 31, on excesses of the prelates: 'Pope Alex. III ordered the bishops not to exercise tithes nor unowed fees against the priests; not to irrationally or dishonestly maltreat them; suspend them without due process; subject their churches to interdict...nor excommunicate them without lawful process...nor can the bishops retain the churches or benefices that were delegated to the priests, because the rights of those giving the powers and those receiving them must be respected'."[141]

Padre Martinez' legal abilities had long since been recognized while under Mexican and now United States administration of New Mexico. He had assisted Governors Donaciano Vigil and James S. Calhoun in several cases and his reputation had grown with his fame.

In July, Martinez went to see Ortiz. Taladrid had left. He and Ortiz made an agreement on dividing the parish duties of Taos. Ortiz made the agreement in writing. Ortiz informed Lamy about their meeting but did not mention the agreement. He only stated, Martinez was continuing to say Mass at the chapels and the padre was getting weaker. He felt the old priest would not be able to continue much longer. Ortiz said he would continue to inform the bishop but that he was beginning to be suspected by his own brothers. He also said, the people were not making their payments to the church. What was he to do about it?

Lamy wrote to Archbishop Kenrick of St. Louis about naming his successor in case of his death. He did not want to take a chance on letting one of the Mexican clergy ascend to the position. The answer to such a problem might lie in the creation of a chapter of cathedral canons for his diocese. He would thus be able to name his successor. Kenrick responded that Barnabo would forward his proposal to Pius IX but that even if his proposal were not approved at Rome

"At least a council of consultors might be created under his archdiocese which would hold authority to act in place of a chapter at Santa Fe, to protect the See of Santa Fe in the event of Lamy's death." [142]

By Autumn of 1857, the sisters had completed their payments to Lamy on the home he had sold them. They were given the deed to "Casa Americana" which they used as a convent. When the sisters arrived in New Mexico he sold it to them for $3,000. The amount was to be paid in three years with the fees they would receive from students attending their school.

On November 10, 1857, Martinez wrote, he had discovered certain abuses by Ortiz. Father Ortiz had told the parishioners, he had the power to collect fees at his discretion, in addition to the tithes. Ortiz threatened them with the denial of the sacraments if they were not paid. In the Sunday sermon of October 29, 1857, at the Church of St. Francis, he again told the parishioners that tithing was not only an ecclesiastical right, but also a divine right. Ortiz stated,

"they would be cast out of the church and even worse, condemned to damnation if the fees were not paid." [143]

Martinez also told Lamy about the written agreement he had with Ortiz concerning the parish duties of Taos. The padre informed Ortiz about his letter to Lamy. Father Eulogio Ortiz denied everything, including his own signature on the agreement. Padre Martinez then wrote to the *Gaceta* repeating his views against enforced tithing and the bishop's disregard of Canon law.

Vicar Juan Felipe Ortiz had returned to America after his illfated trip to the Vatican in April of 1856. The vicar was a thoroughly disheartened and broken man. He continued serving under Bishop Zubiria until his death on January 20, 1858. Vicar Ortiz' death was caused by a sudden loss of consciousness which was the result of an acute vascular lesion of the brain, after he had received the last rites. For three days his body lay in state with hundreds of people passing his bier. The Governor, United States military commander, and the entire legislative assembly payed their last respects to the one "who would be bishop." His requiem Mass was held in the cathedral of St. Francis where he was interred.

March 29, 1858, in a letter to Lamy, Martinez informed the bishop that Eulogio Ortiz had

"committed several sacrilegious acts within the church, had desecrated holy images [wooden Santos], and used profane words which he directed at the Virgin of Guadalupe."

Martinez stated,

"he had been compelled to assume total administration of the parish and that Ortiz was subject to automatic excommunication according to Canon law on sacrilegious acts."[144]

He sent several papers to the bishop outlining the provisions of the Sacred Ministry and of the duties of the ministers of the church.

Cardinal Barnabo had finally convinced the Pope to give Bishop Lamy jurisdiction over the area of Donana. On June 10, 1858, the Vatican wrote to Zubiria expressing their appreciation of his "brilliance of mind and right judgement" but that they were handing control of Donana and Las Cruces to Lamy. Rome, however, made no mention of La Mesilla and the three border towns. These places remained under Zubiria's jurisdiction.

On June 12th, Lamy left Santa Fe to attend another provincial council held by Archbishop Kenrick at St. Louis. The council would convene during the month of September, 1858. Vicar General Machebeuf was left in complete control at Santa Fe.

Father Antoine Avel, one of the French priests, was poisoned on August 3, 1858, while Lamy was in St. Louis. Avel had gone to New Mexico with Lamy in 1854. He had served the Santa Fe parish for a period of four years before being assigned to Mora to replace Father Munnecom as pastor. Lamy and Machebeuf had sent Munnecom, one of the trusted priests brought to New Mexico by the Vicar General, to strengthen the Mora area. The priest's scandalous behavior could not long be ignored so Avel was assigned to replace him. Munnecom, whether through jealousy or anger at being replaced as pastor failed to give the nine o'clock Mass, a few weeks after Avel's arrival. Father Avel was forced to take the absent priest's place. Avel went through the customary sermon and drank some of the wine from the chalice during communion. Apparently noticing a difference in the taste of the wine, he feared he had been poisoned. When certain of it, he gagged out to the congregation,

"Pray for me, I am dying poisoned."[145]

Noel, a man present at Mass, tried frantically to save the priest.

When not finding anything to counteract the poison, it was suggested that Father Munnecom be notified to deliver his last sacraments. Father Avel answered,

"he could not confess to a priest who had poisoned him." [146]

Avel died without receiving the last rites after willing his library and $3,000, so that a hospital could be built, to Bishop Lamy. When Lamy heard of the case from Machebeuf he wrote about Munnecom,

"not a Mexican priest, but an unfortunate Dutch priest..." [147]

Father Munnecom was later cleared of the charge of murder and served out his days as a reassigned pastor until his retirement.

Padre Martinez again declared, the bishop's tithing was without sanction by either Mexican or American law and that it went against the United States Constitution and the teachings of Christ. He wrote a treatise to Lamy which was spread throughout the territory. He stated his sentiments fully and also begged that Lamy should reassess his duties as shepherd of the people.

Padre Martinez' other letters affirmed that his main objection to Bishop Lamy's tactics lay in the manner in which he disregarded established precedent in his enforcement of the collection of church fees. Martinez stated, he had become involved in a dispute regarding tithes as early as 1829. He had protested that they brought heavy obligations upon the poor. As a result of this, they had to bury their dead without proper ceremonies. Many couples were living together without being married and their children went without being Baptized. He wrote a lengthy discourse against the tithing and, aided by other individuals, they were removed in 1833. The precedent was established that church contribution should be made voluntarily rather than by any system of compulsion. Bishop Zubiria regarded the priest's involvement against the tithing as the right of a citizen to express his opinion.

Bishop Lamy, with his reinstatement of the tithes and enforcement of heavy penalties was accused of squeezing money out of the poor. It was felt, Lamy

"would build his cathedral since he was convinced that he could not be regarded as a great servant of the Lord without a proper edifice built in His honor." [148]

His idea was to create a little France in a "wilderness of neglect." [149] Lamy began to replace local church architecture with that patterned after the French. The tithing then became of primary importance for the realization of that dream.

The bishop had begun to recruit French missionaries and in time the following were listed as replacements for the Mexican clergy: (1) Vicar Joseph P. Machebeuf, (2) Rev. Antoine Avel, (3) Rev. Francis Boucard, (4) Rev. N. Bourdier, (5) Rev. N. Carpentier, (6)

Rev. Joseph Coudert, (7) Rev. John B. Courbon, (8) Rev. James Defouri, (9) Rev. Jules Deraches, (10) Rev. Anthony Docher, (11) Rev. Peter Eguillon, (12) Rev. J.B. Faure, (13) Rev. J.B. Fayet, (14) Rev. Joseph Fialon, (15) Rev. Michael Fleurant, (16) Rev. Anthony Fourchegu, (17) Rev. J.B. Francolon, (18) Rev. J. M. Garnier, (19) Rev. Francis Gatignol, (20) Rev. Alex Gourbeyre, (21) Rev. Anthony Jouvenceau, (22) Rev. Francis X Jouvenceau, (23) Rev. N. Jouvet, (24) Rev. George Juillard, (25) Rev. Peter Lassaigne, (26) Rev. Anthony Lamy, (27) Rev. John Latour, (28) Rev. J.B. Mariller, (29) Rev. Philbert Martin, (30) Rev. N. Mathonet, (31) Rev. Munnecom, (32) Rev. Etienne Parisis, (33) Rev. Eugene Paulet, (34) Rev. John Picard, (35) Rev. Francis Pinard, (36) Rev. Clement Peyron, (37) Rev. Henry Pouget, (38) Rev. J. B. Ralliere, (39) Rev. Augustine Redon, (40) Rev. Donato Rogiers, (41) Rev. L. E. Rousset, (42) Rev. J. B. Salpointe, (43) Rev. Camilo Seux, (44) Rev. Augustine Truchard, (45) Rev. Gabriel Ussel, (46) Rev. Augustine Vassal, (47) Rev. Anthony Vermar.

Padre Martinez stated, his case was not a question of heresy or immorality, but rather of the publication of articles criticizing the bishop's tithing. The validity of the bishop's censures became a central point, as Canon law protected the individual cleric against the abuse of authority. Bishop Lamy left himself open to attack in that he admitted, he could not be bothered with legalistic formalities.[150]

During April 10, 1853, the bishop had addressed Purcell:

"...now that I have commenced to reform some abuses and to

lay down a few rules for the clergymen, I have met v. ith a great deal of opposition having been obliged to suspend a few Mexican priests for the most notorious faults; they have submitted but have said that I did not observe the rules prescribed by the Canon law in inflicting these censures. The truth is that if I would comply with all formalities they want, I could never stop the abuses." [151]

Father Peter Eguillon, who had arrived and been ordained in New Mexico in 1854, was appointed vicar general by Lamy. Lamy then sent Machebeuf off to claim Donana on November 3, 1858. The bishop had written to Padre Ramon Ortiz, the vicar forane of the area, saying

"I have received a decree from Rome, whereby Donana and Las Cruces belong to the jurisdiction of Santa Fe. I am sending my Vicar General Sr. Don Jose P. Machebeuf to take possession of the said places. I hope that His Lordship of Durango will have received notice of this matter. I shall be very grateful to you if you will be kind enough to inform the aforementioned vicar of the present situation of these ecclesiastical affairs, and if you would help him, in case any difficulty should arise." [152]

Ramon Ortiz received Machebeuf warmly upon his arrival but could not yield jurisdiction without being informed to do so by his bishop. Arizona had also been given to Lamy in the Vatican decree with the condition that the Bishop of Sonora went along with the transfer of Sonora to Santa Fe. Machebeuf then proceeded to see Bishop Loza in Sonora to inform him of the change. Vicar General Machebeuf left Donana with a detachment of U.S. army troops headed for Arizona. He was successful in finding the bishop after an ardous journey. They met and Machebeuf, as Lamy's representative, asked for the cession of Arizona to the Bishop at Santa Fe. Bishop Loza also ceded La Mesilla and the three contested border towns to Lamy. Although he, as Bishop Odin before him, had no authority to do so. On January 16, 1859, Machebeuf left Sonora armed with his signed documents. He arrived in Santa Fe on March 24, 1859.

There was an immediate response from Bishop Lamy when Vicar General Machebeuf returned to Santa Fe. He wrote in April 1859 to Zubiria informing him that Bishop Loza had given him jurisdiction of La Mesilla and the three border towns. He bluntly stated to the Mexican bishop of Durango, he should now relinquish all rights to the area in question. If he should not, he assured Zubiria,

"I will be obliged to notify the Holy See in Rome of the poor attention given to their Apostolic authority." [153]

In May of 1859, Machebeuf had gone back to Arizona. The bishop from Kansas, J.B. Miege petitioned Rome to assign to Lamy an area of territory under his control. Known as Pike's Peak, the territory then fell right into Lamy's lap. Bishop Lamy, after the undesired surprise, wrote immediately to Barnabo saying he did not care to exercise jurisdiction in Pike's Peak. The Vatican answered Lamy,

"you indicated that you are unable to take any care of the spiritual needs of the Catholics in the territory of Pike's Peak."[154]

Lamy was given Pike's Peak anyway. When the bishop could no longer keep from assuming control of the area he sent for Machebeuf. He returned in the summer very perturbed at having to make the long, hard journey back to Santa Fe.

On June 28, 1859, Zubiria wrote back. He let Lamy know he could not have jurisdiction over La Mesilla. He had ordered his vicar to retain control of the area. The Durango bishop, furthermore, brought to Lamy's attention that he was well aware that the petition from St. Louis sent to Cardinal Barnabo made no mention of La Mesilla; also, Bishop Lamy had attended the synod in St. Louis and had not specified the disputed area; and the Vatican decree did not include the towns. He, therefore, was legitimately the one in authority.

In reference to Lamy's threat of reporting him to the Vatican for his supposed inept administration, Zubiria answered,

"This is not the first time, nor the only proof made to me, of the discreditable image I seem to invite from the first titular Bishop of Santa Fe of New Mexico; however, in Rome, they think very differently of me."[155]

Padre Martinez continued his fight against the tithing. In a letter of September 24, 1859 he declared,

"In all the territory of New Mexico, each year, there are five thousand Baptisms, the fees are as many dollars. Three thousand marriages at eight dollars make twenty-four thousand dollars; burials, three thousand five hundred at six dollars add twenty-one thousand. The patronal feasts given ten thousand dollars and the tithes as much. This means a total of seventy thousand dollars without counting the celebrations and arbitrary fees. But, if the tithes were paid in their entirety it would bring one hundred thousand. And why do the people of New Mexico ignore so exorbitant taxes and complain because the assembly of the territory imposed thirty thousand dollars for the expenses of the territory?"

The priest stated further,

"A fee is given to the minister of religion for the dispensing of the sacraments and other acts of his ministry, and this is very just, for Christ says in St. Matthew's (X-8) the laborer is worthy of his hire. But, this must be understood in a moderate way and spontaneously, and not as a price, as they are exacting the payment of tithes in New Mexico under pain of denying the sacraments, burials, and other offices of the ministry,..."[156]

The Vatican wrote to Lamy,

"As regards the county of Donana, the question is already sufficiently settled and His Eminence, the Prefect of this Congregation has sent his reply to the Bishop of Durango."[157]

Bishop Lamy had already sent Vicar General Peter Eguillon off

to Clermont while Machebeuf was in Sonora. His mission was to recruit more priests in France. On October 27, 1859 the Vicar General arrived in Santa Fe from Clermont with two priests, Jean Baptiste Salpointe, Francis Juvenceau; Deacon John B. Raverdy; four brothers, Hilarien, Gondulph, Geramius and Galmier Joseph; and four pre-seminary students.

By this time, Lamy called Machebeuf in to speak to him.

"I see but one thing to be done,...You have been complaining because I sent for you and have kept you here at Santa Fe—now, don't you see that there was something providential in all this? I do not like to part with you, but you are the only one I have to send, and you are the very man for Pike's Peak."

Machebeuf angrily replied,

"Very well I will go! Give me another priest, some money for our expenses, and we will be ready for the road in twenty-four hours."[158]

Bishop Lamy did not allow Machebeuf to leave until ten months later on September 1860. He assigned Father John B. Raverdy, who had arrived in October of 1859 with his Vicar General Eguillon as a deacon, to accompany Machebeuf. He gave documents to each so that they could present them at their destination. Bishop Jean Baptiste Lamy now had the assistance of Vicar General Eguillon in Santa Fe, and Vicar General Joseph P. Machebeuf in Pike's Peak to help with the administration of his vast diocese.

Padre Martinez continued declaring that the bishop was bound by Canon law. Martinez asserted, he remained as the *parochus proprius* of Taos. The padre felt, he was duty bound to disregard the regulations about tithes and fees and he should try to remedy the damage that was being done by those enforcing them. It was said, Lamy's foreign clergy were keeping as much of said revenue as possible in that they felt the fees were at their discretion.

During the year 1861, Bishop Lamy felt compelled to write to Cardinal Barnabo. Lamy's problem with his enforced tithing were mounting. Padre Martinez' written onslaught against the tithing was gaining momentum. He would have to appeal to Rome for help. Lamy declared to Barnabo,

"Here the principal revenue of the church comes from the tithe. A good number of worshippers give it reluctantly and almost never completely; an even greater number refuse to give it at all. All this makes the administration very difficult. Could we be authorized to change this custom and to adopt rules more suited to our present circumstances, after having consulted our clergy on the matter?"[159]

Bishop Lamy hoped he would now be authorized by the Vatican

to enforce his tithing laws in New Mexico. The custom of voluntary church contributions to be changed to mandatory payment for sacraments through tithes was not very well thought of.

In May of 1861, Bishop Lamy journeyed to a provincial council of bishops held in St. Louis. The council was cancelled because of the outbreak of the American Civil War. Lamy returned to Santa Fe accompanied by six French priests and three French brothers he was able to recruit for his diocese.

The Civil War had a direct impact upon New Mexico. Confederate and Union forces battled for control of the territory. The Southerners took control of Santa Fe for a short period. There was an influx of new people entering the area. A stranger arrived to look the situation over. He was another American bishop, not of the Catholic faith but of the Protestant.

Arriving in 1863, Right Reverend Josiah Cruickshank Talbot of

the Protestant Episcopal Church viewed Santa Fe for the first time. He was ecstatically happy with the growth of the Protestant Church in New Mexico. Bishop Talbot reported he observed,
"loose morals...universal concubinage...open adultery"
everywhere. History was apparently being repeated. Talbot went on to add,
"priests and people alike" were just as guilty. Bishop Talbot felt the Catholic "Church bled the natives for ritual services, including Baptisms, for which, actually, the cathedral bells rang out (for a fee)."[160]
The native New Mexican priests could no longer be criticized. It was now Lamy's own French clergy that were referred to as "immoral and scandalous." Yet Lamy did write later in his life, "Our Mexican population has quite a sad future. Very few of them will be able to follow modern progress. They cannot be compared to the Americans in the way of intellectual liveliness, ordinary skills, and industry; they will thus be scorned and considered an inferior race. If the bishop who will follow me has not lived among the Mexicans for a long time and if he should not show a strong interest in them, they will become disheartened. Seeing themselves on the one hand under American discipline and, on the other, imagining that the Americans prefer foreigners to them, their faith, which is still lively enough, would grow gradually weaker; and the consequences would be dreadful. The morals, manners, and customs of our unfortunate people are quite different from those of the Americans. With the best possible intentions, those who would not try to understand our (native) worshippers or would not become interested in their well-being, would have trouble in adapting to their spirit, which is almost too primitive."[161]

On October 27, 1863, Bishop Lamy left for a pastoral visit to Arizona with a military escort. He was not to return until April 28, 1864. Having left Vicar General Eguillon in charge, he was again informed that the native priests were preparing to report him to Rome. He appealed to Barnabo, saying that seven "miserable priests" he had suspended were sending a petition against him. He asked for the Cardinal's help in the matter. The bishop again asked for La Mesilla and the three border towns in Texas, citing his previous reasons for wanting the area.

Cardinal Barnabo received another letter from Lamy in March of 1865. This time the bishop asked not only La Mesilla, but for Picacho, Los Amoles, La Mesita, La Ysleta and San Elizario to be included in his diocese. Enough funds had been saved with donations and grants to open a hospital to be run by the Sisters of

Charity. The $3,000 Father Avel had provided helped with the hospital funds. Bishop Lamy sold the home behind the cathedral to the nuns. The building was used as the hospital which was opened in January, 1866.

By 1866, Bishop Lamy was required to give an accounting of his administration to the Pope in Rome. He arrived at the Vatican on December 16 and had a private audience with the Holy Father. The bishop reported he had 135 churches, 31 missions, 3 schools operated by the Christian Brothers, 5 schools operated by Loretto Sisters, 1 school operated by Sisters of Charity, he was beginning a seminary and had ordained four students as priests, a hospital and orphanage opened by four sisters of St. Vincent de Paul. He had 51 priests ministering in New Mexico. His census of the territory included: 110,000 Mexicans, 15,000 Indians, 4 to 5,000 Americans, 3 to 4,000 Jews and 30,000 unsettled Indians.

He had made three pastoral visits to Colorado and one to Arizona. He affirmed that he had discovered moral and social abuses caused by the old Mexican clergy. Lamy admitted he could not make regular pastoral visits within his diocese in accordance with Canon law because of the great distances involved, and the constant threat of Indian attacks. The bishop was told to make pastoral visits more often and on a more thorough basis. He should also hold more diocesan synods. Lamy began his journey back to New Mexico on May 9, 1867.

Padre Martinez continued his fight against the bishop's tithes until he fell ill in 1867. The priest had found his health steadily failing him. It seemed to him that his struggle on behalf of his people had been fruitless. The padre felt more dejected as the days passed by. Every appeal to the bishop went unanswered and it seemed that he would never listen to reason. Yet, all of what was taking place seemed to have been prophesied in the priest's past. The padre had written his *Apologia* in 1838 and appeared to have a premonition of what was to occur in his future,

"and if with all this he has yet suffered adversities, he considers himself happy and rejoices in the Lord, when all these things lead him to meditate on those words of the sage, in which, telling about the impious against the just, it says: 'Let us, therefore, lie in wait for the just, because he is not for our turn and is contrary to our doings and upbraideth us with transgressions of the law and divulgeth against us the sins of our way of life...Let us examine him by outrages and tortures...Let us comdemn him to a most shameful death.'[162] But although he has been in the midst of persecutions such as those described, he has not varied his conduct towards all, since he has considered them as a sign of what he is told by

106

Him who believes has sent Him as a minister of the gospel when he says: 'Behold, I send you forth as lambs among wolves. 163 And he has wished to obey the command He has also given him, saying: 'Love your enemies,...do good to them that hate you, and pray for them which despitefully use you and persecute you.' 164 Considering all this, he maintains an inward peace, and an outward frankness and benevolence, he submits to it and protests the continuation of his conduct, and awaits with pleasure what God may send to him, in that glory, accepting it contentedly, even though it be adverse, and to end his days as the Lord shall determine.''

The old padre's present difficulties reflected the words from his past. He thought of the day when he opened his Seminary of Nuestra Senora de Guadalupe in Taos. There had been many young, bright faces amongst his first students that year. They were ready and eager to learn. The padre had spent countless years in study and his photographic memory was brimming with knowledge to pass on to his students. He recalled his sorrow at seeing that the young girls of the villages were receiving no formal education. He found it difficult to convince their parents that their daughters should also attend school. But he did convince them, and the boys took their sisters along with them to the school.

The padre's students, after receiving preparation at his seminary, would complete their training in Durango and receive their ordination. His memory vividly painted the scene of the arrival of his first ordained pupils.

"Padre," they said, "*fue penoso, pero lo hicimos, ahora somos padres tambien.*" (It was hard but we did it, now we are also priests).

The memories brought smiles to his lips. He also thought of the orphans he had raised from childhood. Many had gone on to become priests and tried to follow his good example. Others became statesmen and their governmental abilities carried them well into the American period of New Mexico history. Several foremost legislators, judges, lawyers, theologians, and national delegates were products of the padre's school. Padre Jose Manuel Gallegos, Don Francisco Manzanares, and Anthony Joseph reached the position of delegates to the Congress of the United States and another, Padre Don Antonio Jose Otero, became a Supreme Court Justice in New Mexico. But what of the young girls? Ah, he thought, he had sent some of them to the *conventos* (convents) in Mexico and he hoped they could return some day to their *tierra natal* (native land) as members of a religious order.

His memory lingered from year to year and as it neared the present, his face filled with sorrow. Where were the young native priests that had gone through his school? After his suspension, his students were no longer accepted as candidates for the priesthood. But what happened to those young seminarians that were filled with idealistic dreams when they began their ministry? He thought sadly of those that had resigned, were suspended, or excommunicated because of the bishop's tithing.

> *"Que todo mi trabajo fue por nada?"* (Was all my work in vain?)

he thought.

The padre's illness and reflections filled him with sorrow. He longed to see his wife and child in Paradise and this brought him some consolation. His parishioners, the Brotherhood of Nuestro Padre Jesus Nazareno, his brothers and sisters, tried to console him.

The country doctor, William Kittrige, was called immediately, but there was nothing that he could do.

> *"Todo esta en las manos de Dios,"* (All is in God's hands)

he said to the waiting people.

> "Perhaps the bishop himself will mercifully attend to the padre's sorrow."

Padre Martinez called for a *secretario* (notary) to prepare his last will and testament. The padre noted that he had tried,

> "to the best of my ability to faithfully minister as a clergyman, I have dedicated many years to the effort with eagerness and heart felt devotion to the religious life, to learn to serve my God, my Creator, my Savior."

Thinking about his Catholic religion he said,

> "I have professed its holy truth, and my conscience is quiet and tranquil. God knows that this is true..."

He thought of those that might have misunderstood his good intentions in the past,

> "If there are any of my people that feel that I harmed them, maybe it could have been through a mental error on my part, but not an intention of the heart. The human creature is a fragile one, but I have never had the intention of harming anyone. Naturally, I have always been inclined to do good, and I shall present the testimony of my labor through my deeds: May God help me."

The padre died on July 27, 1867. He repeated his last words, "Thy will be done."[165]

The body of Padre Martinez was laid in state in the *sala* (living room) of his home. Chairs were placed around the room, but all the visitors knelt when reciting the prayers said on his behalf. The *dolientes* (mourners) sat in a different room to receive condolences, and the priest's parishioners took complete charge in the kitchen. The supper served at the *velorio* (wake) was for those who remained all night with the body, and the priest's brothers, sisters, and relatives. His *feligreses* (faithful) kept vigil over his body. *Visitas* (visits) by the brothers of *Neustro Padre Jesus* (the *Penitentes*) were made by members from the *moradas* all over northern New Mexico. One *alabado* would no sooner die down when another group appeared on the scene to pay tribute to *El Conciliador.*[166]

The people united in the courthouse on July 28, 1867 to publicly express their sentiments on the loss of Padre Martinez. Jean Laroux, with tearfilled eyes, addressed the listeners saying,

"He is gone; the priest that served everyone that needed him, with his ministry, his money, and with heartwarming counsel, is gone. No one ever left his side without leaving spiritually richer."

Anthony Joseph praised the padre's life,

"as an exemplary one, worthy of imitation..."

The members of the New Mexico Legislature proclaimed him

"the Honor of his Country."

The whole community assisted at the Mass, but only the men and boys accompanied the body to the *Campo Santo* (cemetary). A priest led the prayers, and the *Penitente rezador* sang the *alabados*. The coffin was carried by Joseph S. Hurst, Anthony Joseph, Henry Stille, Charles Asber, A. Scheurich, Doctor William Kittrige, John Schock, Aniceto Valdez, Juan Francisco Montoya, Vicente Mares, Faustin Trujillo, and Ignacio Pacheco. The padre's brothers and other relatives followed, and the Brothers of *Nuestro Padre Jesus* formed an orderly procession behind them. The remaining participants of the funeral were composed of Americans, Indians from nearby *pueblos,* and the *Hispanos,* all of which totaled more than two thousand.

"When the procession from his home began, a wailing arose and spread from all that accompanied him. In passing Our Lady of Guadalupe Church, they genuflected three times and then a wailing again could be heard." [167]

The procession stopped to rest at intervals. A small cross was raised at these places called *descansos* (rests). Later, short prayers were said at these crosses for the repose of the priest's soul. The *Penitente* brothers sang *alabados* all the way from the church to the burial ground by the chapel, and these could be heard for miles around. The priest was laid to rest at the chapel, and the wailing of the people grew with each spadeful of earth cast upon the *sepulcro* (sepulcher).

Padre Martinez had not been a soldier with armor of metal, strong lance and tempered sword, but simply, a soldier of Christ.

109

His armor was his faith, and his weapons, a crucifix, a rosary, and a small book of prayers. With these he conquered hundreds of souls and he was respected and loved by *Hispanos*, Americans, and the Indians, who revered him as a 'Holy Man' with infinite power.

He was the supporter and the protector of all his people. His smile and words rekindled the hopes of those valiant Southwestern people, and that is why in the moment that they had lost him forever, they cried without consolation.

They prayed for him and dedicated a final memory before returning to their homes.

Lamy returned to New Mexico from his accounting to the Vatican on August 15, 1867. He arrived with several more priests that he had recruited. A small group of nuns also accompanied him back to Santa Fe. The bishop heard of the death of Padre Martinez, but made no response.

Bishop Lamy went on to distinguish himself as a valiant church leader in the Southwest. His long career spanned across half a century, and upon his retirement he wrote,

"For some years past we had asked of the Holy See a coadjutor in order to be relieved of the great responsibility that rested on our shoulders since the year 1850, when the supreme authority of the Church saw fit to establish a new diocese in New Mexico, and in spite of our limited capacity we were appointed its first Bishop. Now our petition has been heard and our resignation accepted. We are glad, then, to have as a successor the Illustrious Mons. Salpointe, who is well known in this bishopric, and worthy of administering it, for the good of the souls and the greatest glory of God.

"What has prompted this determination is our advanced age, that often deprives us of the necessary strength in the fulfillment of our sacred ministry, though our health may apparently look robust. We shall profit by the days left to us to prepare ourselves the better to appear before the tribunal of God, in tranquility and solitude.

"We commend ourselves to the prayers of all, and particularly those of our priests who, together with us have borne and still bear the burden of the day, which is the great responsibility of directing the souls in the road of salvation. Let the latter remember that, in order that their holy ministry be of any benefit, their example must accompany their instructions. It is with pleasure that we congratulate the most of the clergy of this diocese for their zeal and labors; and we desire those who might have failed in their sacred duties may give, henceforth, better proofs of being the worthy ministers of God.

"We also commend ourselves to the prayers of the faithful, whose lively faith has edified us on many an occasion. We exhort them to persevere in this same faith, in their obedience to the Church, in their faithfulness to their daily obligations, in the religious frequence of the Sacraments and in the devotion to the Blessed Virgin Mary, which is one of the most efficacious means of sanctification.

"Finally, we hope that the few religious communities we have had the happiness to establish in this new diocese will offer some memento in their prayers for our spiritual benefit. "We ask of all to forgive us the faults we may have committed in the exercise of our sacred ministry, and, on our part, we will not forget the offer to God our humble prayers for all the souls that the Lord has entrusted to us for so many years. J. B. LAMY, ARCHBISHOP". [168]

Archbishop Jean Baptiste Lamy died on February the 13th, 1888.

"Just as Jesus patiently suffered injustice, calumny, abuse and physical torture, so too we must make an effort to accept the hardships and pains and trials and misfortunes of life, and even to embrace voluntary privations and sacrifices, with something of His gentleness, humility and love."

—Thomas Merton, *Bread in the Wilderness* (New Direction)

Epilogue

Willa Cather in *Death Comes for the Archbishop* chose to make Lamy, in the character of Bishop Latour, a virtuous hero and the notable Padre Martinez, a villain of the worst kind. Padre Martinez' purpose in promoting education among his people had been so that they could retain their cultural identity and compete in an advancing society. The bishop in his unconcern for that identity, does not emerge as the kind, patient, mild mannered character portrayed by many authors. Nor does the priest appear as the "lecherous ogre" portrayed by sensational writers.

Many vanity histories and biographies have been written mentioning the priest. One writer says the priest was legitimately married to one Teodora Romero and they had a rather large family. [169] In fact, Teodora Romero was the wife of one of the padre's brothers and they did have a large family. [170] But, the Martinez name was legion in the church records of Taos with similar name combinations; Antonio, Jose Antonio, or Antonio Jose. This may account for the stories that the priest had a harem and most of his descendants were proud to acknowledge his paternity. He was also accused of having countless incestuous love affairs, i.e. Willa Cather. Of course one writer says that other priests of his day had harems and committed highly immoral spiritual incest. [171]

Concerning one of the orphans, Santiago Valdez, that Padre Martinez had raised, the priest did emphasize in his testament of June 27, 1867,

> "I have from his *infancy* taken care of him and adopted him with all the privileges and educated him...He has not recognized any other father and mother but me, and besides he has been obedient to me; for this reason I depose and it is my will that *his sons* take and carry *my surname* in the future." [172]

In the course of time, it might have been forgotten that the priest had not been Santiago's actual father.

In 1857, Bishop Lamy brought his niece, Marie Lamy to Santa Fe to join him. Many later falsely claimed that she was in reality his illegitimate daughter. The sensational stories, enlarged by others, hurt the integrity of both men and twisted the truth of the excommunication of Padre Martinez out of proportion.

There is an undated letter in the file on Padre Martinez in the Archdiocesan archives. It was written by a Dolores Perea of Isleta, and she informs Bishop Lamy,

"of the scandals Padre Martinez is causing by having a woman of bad fame in the community as his housekeeper."

Padre Antonio Jose Martinez was, however, never stationed at Isleta. But a French priest, Rev. Philbert Martin, was there between 1854-1856 when he was replaced by Taladrid. It was natural for the Perea woman to refer to the priest as Padre Martinez rendering the French name into the common Spanish one.

Padre Martinez' connections with the *Penitente* Brotherhood has been the subject of much conjecture. The origins of the lay society in New Mexico does lie in obscurity, but certain circumstantial evidence can be taken into account.

The Third Order became firmly entrenched in New Mexico, almost at the beginning, with the establishment of two chapels. One was situated in Santa Fe, and the other in Santa Cruz. It continued to grow until the independence of Mexico from Spain brought it to a decline and an inevitable end. This was not due to a lack of priestly leadership as most historians have wrongfully surmised, but for the introduction of another society which steadily took its place. Many of the Franciscan priests were recalled after the independence of Mexico. The Third Order, temporarily, found itself without spiritual guidance. However, a native priest by the name of Antonio Jose Martinez, who had been studying in Durango, Mexico, returned to New Mexico in February 1823. By 1826 he had been assigned to the heavily concentrated Third Order area of Santa Cruz as curate of Abiquiu and Taos and most significantly as Delegate Minister of the Third Order.

Padre Martinez began to travel throughout the area, saying Mass in Santa Cruz (more than likely in the Third Order Chapel), and conducting Holy Week services in Santa Fe. It is generally believed that he was the only priest assigned as Third Order Minister at this critical time in its existence. No other records are known of any one else being given the delegation. It is also significant that it was given him as a personal delegation and not as one in keeping with his functions as a priest. This alone makes it highly improbable that any other priest served as a minister of the Third Order at this time.

He was soon recognized as the Superior or *Supremo* of *La Hermandad* which in time supplanted the Third Order. Many have over-looked his association with the Third Order while others have continuously wondered as to why the Third Order declined and faded although the energetic priest of Taos was its leader. Padre Martinez dedicated himself with extraordinary perseverance to any task or goal, whether assigned or voluntary, and that given him as Third Order minister would have received no less of a dedication. But, as tradition states, he organized the extant societies into a unified whole as *El Conciliador*, and founded La Hermandad de Padre Jesus in New Mexico. *La Hermandad* kept the religious zeal of Spain's past alive in New Mexico and the heritage from the beginning was kept intact and handed down through the years.

Padre Martinez is credited with having written the religious dramatization, sermons, and dialogue, of Holy Week for the *Penitentes*. On Holy Friday, the *Penitentes* held the *Sermon de la Manana* (morning sermon) which was a sacramental dramatization of the Passion of Christ. This generally followed the morning Mass. The *Sermon de la Tarde* (afternoon sermon) took place in the *patio* of the *Morada* (chapel). Pilate and the Centurions were grouped about *El Cristo Crucificado*, a life sized wooden statue of Christ on the Cross. The Brothers of Light took the parts of the principal characters of the drama, and a small girl was Veronica. During the performance of the religious dramatization, the Brothers of Blood remained within the *Morada* to do penance. The cracking of the whips accompanied by the shrill notes of the *pitos* (flutes) and clacking of the *matracas* (noise makers) could be heard until the termination of the drama. A long narrative hymn which retold the whole history of Christ's trial and crucifixion had been read earlier. At the end the *Cristo bulto* (Christ's figure) was carefully lowered from the cross by the *Hermanos* (brothers) and placed in a coffin which was then carried in procession. After a short walk, the public participants withdrew to their homes and the Brothers returned to the *Morada*. [173]

It is the opinion of a noted historian that the priest may have provided the organizational terminology for the *Penitente* Brotherhood from his previous studies in Mexico. [174]

Padre Martinez himself, another writer states, may also have provided the inspiration for a famous *santero's* (religious image maker) work through his studies in Mexico where he could have seen illustrated manuscripts and described them to the *santero*. [175] The priest's influence upon New Mexico's *Penitentes* and *santeros* could have been very great indeed, with the development of the *Jesus Nazarenos*, *Virgen Dolorosas*, and religious dramatizations.

Another persistent rumor which occurs to this day concerns Padre Martinez' obtaining of a grant of land from the Taos Indians. It is said, he never paid for the land. However, it is a proven fact that the Indians approached Padre Martinez before 1845 saying that they needed money. The priest stated,

"as wards of the Mexican government you have to secure permission to sell the land; otherwise, you cannot do so."

The Indians did secure the necessary papers and were allowed to sell. The whole affair became a matter of record on April 26, 1847, according to Book A, page 54, in the Surveyor General's office.

The consideration was $532.05, and the document was signed by five Indians and witnessed by Santiago Martinez and F. P. Blair. [176]

Bishop Lamy's removal of the native clergy was tragic. The opinion was formed that New Mexicans were neither educationally nor morally fit for the priesthood. It deprived the Hispanic New Mexicans of their leaders, leaving a "wound that was long to heal and a scar that can still be felt."

The Catholic Apostolic Christian Church

by

Padre Antonio Jose Martinez

The Christian Church, according to the attributes or predicates given in the above title was the Primitive Church of that religion which the apostles preached, established and founded by the command of its author, Jesus Christ. There was no hierarchy (the Pope, Cardinals, Primates, Patriarchs, Archbishops, Bishops, etc., compose the hierarchy in the Roman Church, to say nothing of their revenues) amongst them, they were all equal, and none was greater than the other, for so the Lord commanded them in the Gospel of Matthew 20:26-27. Their treatment of each other was that of brethren: St. Peter in his first Epistle 2:15 treats Paul as a brother.

Their duty, according to their Lord's order, was to preach the Gospel, teaching and indoctrinating the peoples in the faith of God, in the Incarnation of the Divine Word in the words of sound morality—the commandments of the Law of God, Exodus 20; in the immortality of the soul of the children of the human race and in the practice of righteousness, in order to escape hell and gain a right to obtain eternal happiness in Jesus Christ.

Church. This word comes from assembly, that is, a union of many persons in the same place, to treat of matters important to the public good. In this sense the Israelites said to Moses, Num. 20:4: "Why have ye brought the Assembly (church) of the Lord into this wilderness?" and Christ, speaking of brotherly correction, says: "If he hear not the Church, let him be unto thee as a Gentile and a Publican." Mat. 18:17. This is the same understanding of the word given by the Apostles to the congregations of the faithful, as St. John in Rev. 1:4 to the seven churches in Asia. So it is clear that it is called Christian Church after Christ, its Author, and the head of its religion since every congregation of the faithful who in the name of Christ are assembled, treated and governed in the hope of obtaining spiritual salvation is called Christian or a Christian church. This pertains as well to the church of the Roman communion as to the Greek, the Lutheran and the various reformed churches called Protestant, because they have protested against abuses that have been

116

committed, who uniformly follow faith in God and in Jesus Christ, and practice religion in the morality established by Christ and his Apostles; as Paul says, Ephe. 2:30, "built on the foundation of the Apostles and Prophets, Jesus Christ himself being the chief corner stone." To these churches belongs the epithet of Apostolic. Such of these as follow the same rule in their form and ceremonies should be called, and are, particular churches; but the aggregate of them all, that is, the Roman, the Greek, the Lutheran, and the rest that acknowledge and worship Christ, though they differ in ceremonies, from the Catholic or Universal Church, as they preserve unity with Christ in Faith and practices.

The Roman church at its beginning, gained the attention of the whole Catholic world, and accumulated power in proportion to the acquiescence of the rest of the churches; but at length, with the establishment of the crusaders, of the Tribunal of the Holy Inquisition of canonical punishments, of the bulls of crusading, of dispensations and others that sold indulgences and benefits to the people for weighty pecuniary items, and especially with the acquisition of temporal power, it indulged to such an extent in committing excesses, abusing the authority and supremacy that the peoples, Kings and Emperors gave her, that in this one reason emerged for the divisions that today cover the world with Apostolic Christians, who, although not Roman ones, yet far outnumber those who acknowledge Rome. (In genuine history there are thirty-nine millions more Christians in the churches that do not acknowledge Rome than there are in her fold.) Hence, it turns out that the unity, infallibility and defense afforded by the famous Gospel "on this Rock will I build my Church, and the Gates of Hell shall not prevail against it" have failed to be fulfilled in the Roman church, as it has not made it the exclusively Christian church. Therefore, either the gates of Hell have prevailed and that promise has failed; or else, said promise belongs to all Christian churches, and as a consequence the Roman church is only a particular church, when speaking of the Church of Christ, and the term Catholic or Universal belongs to the assemblage of all the above mentioned churches. In this way unity is preserved, and the Savior's promise is fulfilled.

Unity, I say, for although they differ in the ceremonies, which are accidental to religion, they preserve Unity, which is important and essential. Paul Ep. to Ephesians 4:1-16; Unity in the faith is one only God and in Jesus Christ, in the only Baptism by which the faithful are enrolled and characterized as sons of God and united in the bonds of peace to follow truth with love, firm and efficacious hope which unites us to Christ, who is head of all, gathering all up into one body to inherit eternal bliss.

The promise is being fulfilled, because the number of believing Christians in the particular churches is not diminished but rather

117

increases and strengthens the faith by the preaching of the Gospel, and thus it is that it may be truly said: "On this Rock will I build my Church, Mat. 16:18, And the gates of Hell shall not prevail against it."

This is the Universal Church which bears each of the marks which distinguish it-to-wit: infallibility in the mysteries of the faith, and regularity in morality.

Infallibility is one of the cardinal points in the Church of Christ, and this is not found in the will of man nor in the scope of human knowledge, but only in divine revelation. II Peter 1:19-21. We can and ought to read Holy Scriptures, to reap spiritual fruit from them, since we have for this the express command of the Lord in John 5:39. "Search the Scriptures, etc.," and St. Paul in Rome 15:4, says: "For all things written in the past, were written for our instruction so that we might have hope through patience and the comfort of the Scriptures." These in the Church are the "pillar and ground of truth." I Tim. 3:15. "It is written in the Prophets: all shall be taught of God." John 6:45. See then, how the Scriptures given by Divine revelation are the final tribunal and the fundamental support in the Church of Christ. The Roman church in its operation is manifested in the statutes of Popes and Councils, which repeal and contradict what each other decrees. Hence, it is only infallible when its decision agrees with Holy Scripture. Therefore, the universal Church of Christ has its infallibility in the said Scriptures, and thus the promises are fulfilled.

Another cardinal point very important in the Church of Christ, is what should be believed, and the work of righteousness, or sound morality. All should believe the existence of God, the Author of Creation, that He is a just rewarder, recompensing the good and punishing the evil; that He is infinitely wise, true, powerful, eternal, provident, and thus absolute in all his other attributes; the Trinity of the Persons, Father, Son and Holy Spirit, and one only God; the incarnation of the divine Word, the Second Person to redeem the world from original sin which passed to the sons from the sin of their first parents, and from personal sins; that Christ, as man was conceived by the Virgin Mary and born of her, not by connections with man but by the Holy Spirit, to whom love is attributed by the valuation of the Angel Gabriel. Luke 1:28-38. Finally, all should believe that he preached His doctrine, wrought miracles to confirm the same, suffered persecution and torment even unto death and was nailed to the shameful cross; which sacrifice that finished his mission to the world was offered to the Eternal Father for all men; that he arose on the third day and conversed with his disciples until the day of his ascension to Heaven; with the rest that is taught in Holy Scripture.

As to morality, St. Augustine, Doctor of the Church, says: "Natural law is the very reason or will of God, which commands us to preserve the natural order, and forbids us to disturb it." This includes the observance of the ten commandments of the Law of God, and is the practice of works of righteousness and virtue. Christ taught this doctrine and commanded his Apostles to preach it. Mat. 28:18-20. "All authority in Heaven and on Earth has been given to me; go, therefore, and teach all nations, Baptizing them in the name of the Father, and of the Son, and of the Holy Spirit; teaching them to observe all things which I have commanded you."

It is proper that there should be Gospel Ministers in the Church of Christ, as successors in the office of the Apostles and elders, to carry the preaching of the Gospel to the peoples. Acts 20:28. "Take heed to yourselves and to the flock, over which the Holy Spirit has made you bishop to feed the Church of God which he bought with his blood."

The Apostles faithfully fulfilled the command of Christ, all were martyrs, and sealed with their blood the doctrine they published, scattered among the nations to preach the Gospel; and we, the ministers of today, are likewise obligated to do now; but importunately we observe that several Ministers of the Roman communion in New Mexico refuse to administer sacraments, burying in consecrated ground and other services of their ministry, unless all the tithes, first fruits, fees and other duties are paid in full, and even force voluntary contributions to a higher figure than that proposed by the devotees. Such traffic is identical with the chaffering of pawnbrokers and auctioneers; this practice is contrary to what Jesus Christ commanded in Mat. 10:8-10, which the apostle and the ministers of the primitive church observed. That church was truly Apostolic; but on the contrary, we see what was prophesied in Acts 20:29 happening. "I know that after my departure grievous wolves will attack you, which will not spare the flock." See 2 Peter, 2:1-3 "of a truth there were false Prophets***as also there will be false treachery among you; deceivers who will introduce destructive heresies and will deny the Lord who bought them*** And many will follow them in their lascivious doings*** and with feigned words will make traffic of you for avarice." Is not this what is now commonly happening in those who follow the observance of a diocesan decree of January 14, 1854, making merchandise of the graces and services of the Ministry? We see this with deep pain, and the ignorance of the people and their abject condition are not moved by words of the Gospel that exhort them to know the truth.

To conclude: We affirm that the Catholic and Universal Church of Christ possesses the promise of being infallible in the Holy Scripture that is the pillar and ground of the truth, in which the immortality of our soul and the promise of eternal happiness is found. Read the word of God contained in the Holy Bible and ponder the true and just maxims of this divine teacher. If we do this, the Holy Spirit will illumine us with his gifts and will impel us by the flame of his love, so that we may walk in the right way, and at the end of our days, by the will of final perseverance, we shall attain unto eternal life. Amen.

ANTONIO JOSE MARTINEZ DE SANTISTEVAN

"When it comes to the public testimony of the faith for just the ordinary Catholic in just ordinary circumstances a few points should be kept in mind. For the most part people outside the Church are not too benevolently disposed to the man-made aspects of the Catholic Church. The public testimony of the Faith has to be on more essential points of Christianity, more genuinely a Christian article. The beatitudes would be a good starting place. In an age when greed is the rage and possessions are the badge of distinction, it takes courage to live publicly 'poor in spirit.' But the Christian who has the courage of his convictions and actually lives up to this beatitude will give as big a jolt to his environment as any martyr in a Roman arena.

"The best advertisement is a satisfied customer. The Christian way of life has never been the most comfortable way of life. It has always demanded a certain amount of heroic virtue in every age. And the man who has the courage to live that way of life joyfully in twentieth-century America is the man who is going to bring America to Christ."

—Daniel Fearon, O.P., *Graceful Living* (Newman)

BASILICA OF OUR LADY OF SORROWS
Chicago, Illinois
CANON LAW OF THE CHURCH
AND
EXCOMMUNICATION
by
Father Alberto Gallegos, O.S.M., S.T.L.

Like every other society, the Catholic Church also has its laws. Church Law is called Canon Law. The purpose of the law is to help organize and direct the principal activities entrusted to that Church by its founder, namely the preaching of the message of the Good News and aiding in the orderly dispensing of the sacramental life of that Church. The sacraments are distinctive marks of the Catholic Church. Canon law defines the rights and duties of the members of the Catholic Church.

Canon law helps maintain uniformity so that the essential makeup of the Church may be kept intact. At the same time, it allows for exceptions and particular needs and conditions as to place and time in particular historical settings. The Church has its proper life but only in as far as it affects its members. The Holy Spirit, it must be remembered, is working in and through each living member of that Community. The laws of the Church must allow for putting the inspirations of the Holy Spirit to the test. Since essential growth of the Spirit comes from within, through the workings of grace and that Spirit—laws are primarily concerned with external activity—it must likewise be remembered that the life of the Church considers also the Christian's, "Life in Grace."

Church Penalties

An ecclesiastical penalty is the privation of some good inflicted by legitimate authority on the delinquent for his correction and for punishment of the offense (Canon 2215). There are three (3) kinds of penalties in the Catholic Church: 1. Corrective punishments or censures, 2. Punitive Penalties, 3. Penal Remedies and Penances (Canon 2216).

In the infliction of penalties, the punishment must be in just proportion to the offense. It must have due regard to the amount of responsibility, scandal, and damage. Attention must be paid to the age, knowledge, sex, state of life, condition of mind, and dignity of the person against whom the crime is committed. The crime must be certified as a crime according to the same Canon Law.

It must be assertained whether the offender acted under the influence of passion, or out of fear, whether he repented and tried himself to prevent its evil consequences. Circumstances which excuse from all sin, also those excusing from Grave sin do likewise excuse from incurring any penalty whether *"latae or ferendae sententiae,;"* the excuse holds also in the external form if the mitigating circumstances can be proved. No penalty can be inflicted unless it is certain that the offense was committed and that legitimate prescription had been enterned against it.

Censures

A censure is a penalty by which a subject of the Church is deprived of some spiritual benefit or benefits that have to do with spiritual matters. Canon law tells us that Censures and especially Excommunication should be inflicted very rarely and with great prudence. (Canon 2241) Only those external criminal actions that are grave sins, complete, and committed with obstinacy should be punished with censures. There are certain canonical admonitions that must be observed before any censure can be given.

Infliction of Penalties

The words of Canon Law are very clear and state clearly what the condition must be for severe censures:

"No penalty can be inflicted unless it is certain a crime has been committed and that its prosecution is not barred by prescription (canon 223#1). Even though it is legally proved, if there is question of inflicting a censure, the culprit must be reprehended and warned to desist from contumacy according to Canon 2242#3, and if in the prudent judgment of the same judge, or superior, it seems fitting, a suitable time should be allowed him to comply; if the contumacy continues, the censure may be inflicted. (Canon Law 2233...)"

There are three (3) censures according to Canon Law: (1) Excommunication, (2) Interdict, (3) Suspension. Excommunication can fall only on a real person. We call that a Moral Person. Both interdict and suspension may be imposed on a community as a legal person; interdict and excommunication affect also lay persons; suspension is a penalty for clerics only. Interdict may also effect a place. An excommunication is always a censure. Interdict and suspension may be either censures or punitive penalties. In case of doubt, (canon 2225) they are considered censures.

123

Excommunication

The most severe penalty which the Church can inflict on one of its members is excommunication. It is cutting off the ties that bind us together. It is exclusion from Communion and with communion with the rest of the faithful. The effects are enumerated in Canons 1543 to 1551. It is also called "anathema"! If it is inflicted with the formalities described in the Pontificale Romanum, it is a most rigid and death-like thing (Canon 2257).

The excommunicated person may be either *Excommicati Vitandi* or *Excommicati Tolerati.* No one is excommunicated "Vitandus" unless he has been excommunicated by name by the Holy See, has been publically denounced as such, and explicitly declared a "Vitandus" in the Vatican Decree or Canonical Sentence.

Every excommunicated person is deprived of the right to assist at Divine Offices but can be present at Sermons (Office is the official prayer of the Church. Each priest is bound to say office daily). Every excommunicated person is forbidden to receive the Sacraments (there are seven (7) enumerated in the Catholic Church). An excommunicated priest is forbidden to celebrate Mass and to administer the sacraments and sacramentals (giving ashes, blessing throats, blessing rosary beads). However, the faithful may, for a good reason ask the excommunicated if there is no other minister around, to administer the sacraments for them. An excommunicated priest may always administer sacraments in danger of death. An excommunicated priest is deprived of indulgencies, public prayers and suffrages of the Church.

PADRE MARTINEZ was a man ahead of his time but lived very much in his own time. Who is to be the judge as regards to his soul? Only God obviously. We can only ask ourselves some questions and make up our own mind. It is the opinion of this writer that Padre Martinez was not excommunicated according to the norms of Canon Law. His ministry was valid at all times. Bishop Lamy himself admitted that he had not followed Canon Law faithfully during that excommunication. In retrospect, we of the 20th Century look back and see so many more things that affected the two men. One can ask the following questions in trying to reach a personal decision as regards to the excommunication of the priest:

1. Did Padre Martinez commit a real crime?

2. Was there ever a question in officials heads that they were making a big mistake?

3. Were all the canonical "warnings" given and was there given sufficient time to react and retract?

4. Was the padre's age and service considered in the evaluation?

5. Was he excommunicated *Vitandi or Tolerati?*

In summation, this writer must reiterate that the excommunication of Padre Antonio Jose Martinez was not conducted according to Canon law and because of that fact his excommunication was, and always has been, illegal and invalid.

Memorial

Albuquerque, New Mexico

April 22, 1976

The life story of Padre Antonio Jose Martinez, very clearly points out the great Hermano Conciliador he was. We the Hermanos of Jesus Nazareno are still enjoying the fruits of his toil.

I, the Hermano Supremo Arzobispal, feel that his name should be completely vindicated from all charges brought against him during his administration and his unjust excommunication lifted.

The story of Padre Martinez and Bishop Lamy proves that the humble priest was a victim of circumstances.

M. SANTOS MELENDEZ,
HERMANO SUPREMO ARZOBISPAL

Acknowledgements

The completion of this work on Padre Martinez and Bishop Lamy is through the efforts of many that have offered help and encouragement through the years. I first went to Sister Paulinia, former head librarian of the University of Albuquerque, in 1968 with my thought of writing about the great historical conflict. I had just finished reading *Death Comes for the Archbishop*. I wanted to find out for myself what had actually happened between the priest and the bishop.

Sister Paulinia's patience and understanding of the seemingly insurmountable problem served as an inspiration to search on. Another dear friend, Sister Lauriana, continuously prompted me to try harder and strive to find every piece of documentation that would support my thesis concerning the excommunication. Others at the time that aided my effort in some way were: Dr. Jorge Alarcon, Theodore Foss, Warren Lee, Sister Joella Revers, John Archibeque and Dr. James McGrath.

I am greatly indebted to M. Santos Melendez, the present Supremo of the Brotherhood of *Nuestro Padre Jesus*. He has been of constant counsel and help in the final stages of this work and his encouragement is realized with its completion.

I am indebted to Mrs. Dora Martinez de Armijo, the grandniece of Padre Martinez and granddaughter of Pascual Martinez. She spent countless hours recounting her reminiscenses and recollections of stories she had heard first hand from her parents. She was very concerned with the misinformation that arose due to Willa Cather's book, *Death Comes for the Archbishop*. She also sought to encourage the completion of this book.

The librarians at Carnegie Library in Las Vegas, New Mexico deserve an extra note of appreciation. Mary Valdez, Southwest Librarian, Sharon Jiron, Interlibrary Loan and Eileen Eshner sought every piece of information I requested and provided all the services of the library to me.

I am also indebted to Virginia Jennings of the New Mexico State Library for her initial compilation of a bibliography on Padre Martinez.

Special thanks is given to Dr. Myra Ellen Jenkins, Chief of the Historical Services Division of the New Mexico State Records

Center and Archives, and State Historian for providing assistance with many of the microfilm originals of the letters appearing in this volume, and her interest and research on the banner.

As to the New Mexico banner, I am greatly appreciative to Mike Weber and Mike Cox of the Museum of New Mexico, Dr. J.J. Brody and Dr. Stout of the Maxwell Museum of Anthropology at the University of New Mexico. Also, Dr. Claudio Estevan Fabregat of the Anthropology Department of the University of Barcelona, Spain, for their involved interest in trying to provide more information to me as to its origin and meaning other than folk and family tradition. Mr. Raymond N. Rogers of the University of California—Los Alamos Scientific Laboratory, also spent countless hours in analyzing the flag's dyes and fibers in a comprehensive study.

A special note of appreciation is extended to Mr. Joe Robert Sanchez and Dr. Jose R. Lopez-Gaston for their encouragement and Fray Angelico Chavez; Padre Benedicto Cuesta; Dr. Bainbridge Bunting; Richard Federici; Howard Bryan; Jack K. Boyer, Director of the Kit Carson Museum; Fred Martinez; Father Auman, Immaculate Conception Church, Tome, New Mexico; Father J. Sabine Griego, Our Lady of Sorrows Church, Las Vegas, New Mexico; Ruben Dario Salaz, Editor, Blue Feather Press; Archbishop Roberto F. Sanchez, Archbishop of Santa Fe; Carol Tinker, Director of the Las Vegas Chamber of Commerce; Richard Salazar, New Mexico Records and Archives, Santa Fe; and Arthur Olivas, Photo Records, Museum of New Mexico for their aid and information.

I sincerely appreciate the help of Father Alberto Gallegos for his writing on the Canon law of the Church.

Footnotes

1. Ralph Emerson Twitchell, *Old Santa Fe*, pp. 11-13.
2. Abiquiu was originally founded as a genizaro village (a town for Indians from various tribes). However, in 1747 it was destroyed by the Utes with no survivors recorded. The area was later resettled by Spanish colonists.
3. Aurora Lucero White, *Los Hispanos*, pp. 29-30.
4. Ibid., pp. 9-12
5. El Historiador (pen name), *Historia Consisa del Cura de Taos*, Antonio Jose Martinez, Taos, New Mexico, 1861.
6. Fanny Calderon de la Barca, *Life in Mexico*.
7. Archives of the Archdiocese of Santa Fe cited in the notes will be referred to as A.A.S.F., L.D. 1815, No. 21.
8. A.A.S.F. Accounts, LXIV, Box 5-E, Visitation of Agustin Fernandez de San Vicente,, 1826.
9. A.A.S.F., L.D. 1827, No. 10
10. Pedro Sanchez, *Memorias Sobre la Vida del Presbitero, Don Antonio Jose Martinez*, pp. 17-19.
11. A.A.S.F., Patentes, Book 70, 1831.
12. Pedro Sanchez, *Memorias Sobre la Vida del Presbitero, Don Antonio Jose Martinez*, p. 20.
13. Previous Vicar General under Bishop Castaniza.
14. Huntington Library, William G. Ritch notes (1846-1896), Memo Book No. 4, p. 325.
15. Ibid.
16. Pedro Sanchez, *Memorias Sobre la Vida del Presbitero, Don Antonio Jose Martinez*, p. 30.
17. Ralph Emerson Twitchell, ed., *Old Santa Fe*, Vol. II, 1914-15, (Old Santa Fe Press), pp. 4 & 5.
18. Ralph E. Twitchell, ed., *Leading Facts of New Mexico History*, Vol. II, p. 64.
19. F. Edward Hulme. *The History, Principles and Practice of Heraldry*, pp. 133-134.
20. Pedro Sanchez, *Memorias Sobre la Vida del Presbitero, Don Antonio Jose Martinez*, p. 24.
21. The term *genizaro* was used as a derogatory remark. In essence, it meant a man without a land or country. As Benedict Arnold was a *genizaro* in the U.S. so was Gonzales a *genizaro* in New Mexico. Armijo did not fail in using it as such. However, later historians, in failing to realize that the term had a double meaning, established that Gonzales must have been a full blooded Indian. This was also an attempt at portraying the revolutionaries as a wild, savage, and illiterate mob intent on murder and pillage of the land. In fact it was a well planned and disciplined attempt to overthrow what was believed to be a tyrannical government imposed by Mexico. General Gonzales may have had some Indian blood which could have served to unite New Mexico's racial elements. But this, however, is a matter of conjecture rather than factual evidence. Gonzales, as records indicate, was a highly educated man.
22. Eric M. Odendahl, *Saint or Devil?*, (True West Magazine, March, April, 1967) pp. 34 & 66.
23. Paul Horgan, *Lamy of Santa Fe*, (N.Y., 1975), p. 41.
24. Aurelio M. Espinosa and J. Manuel Espinosa, *The Texans: A New Mexican Folk Play of the Middle Nineteenth Century*, (New Mexico Quarterly Review, Autumn 1943, Vol. XIII, No. 3, pp. 299-308.)
25. Paul Horgan, *Lamy of Santa Fe*, (N.Y., 1975), pp. 42-43.
26. Ibid., p. 43
27. David Lavender, *Bent's Fort*, (1954), p. 275.
28. Paul Horgan, *Lamy of Santa Fe*, (N.Y., 1975), pp. 45-46
29. R.E. Twitchell, ed., *Old Santa Fe*, Vol. 2, 1914-1915, p. 256.
30. R.E. Twitchell, ed. *Old Santa Fe*, Vol. 1, Oct. 1913, p. 255.
31. R.E. Twitchell, *History of the Military Occupation of the Territory of New Mexico*, pp. 240-241.
32. Paul Horgan, *Lamy of Santa Fe*. (N.Y., 1975), p. 55.
33. Ibid., p. 56
34. Pedro Sanchez, *Memorias Sobre la Vida del Presbitero, Don Antonio Jose Martinez*, p. 20.

35. Paul Horgan, *Lamy of Santa Fe,* (N.Y., 1975), p. 59.
36. Ibid., p. 59
37. Ibid., p. 66.
38. Richard E. Ahlborn, *The Penitente Moradas of Abiquiu,* p. 126.
39. George Wilkins Kendall, *Narrative of the Texan-Santa Fe Expedition,* p. 46.
40. Paul Horgan, *Lamy of Santa Fe,* (N.Y., 1975), p. 126.
41. Ibid., p. 128.
42. Ibid., p. 74
43. Ibid.
44. Ibid., p. 90
45. Ibid., pp. 91-93
46. Ibid., p. 99
47. Ibid., p. 106.
48. Ibid., pp. 107-108.
49. Letter of August 15, 1851 (Notre Dame) Lamy to Archbishop Anthony Blanc of New Orleans.
50. R.E. Twitchell, *Old Santa Fe,* Vol. 1, Oct. 1913, p. 178.
51. Rev. Jean Baptiste Salpointe, *Soldiers of the Cross,* p. 179.
52. Treatise in Library of Congress, New Mexico Archives, *Recollections of the Life of the Priest, Don Antonio Jose Martinez,* Pedro Sanchez, p. 18.
53. Paul Horgan, *Lamy of Santa Fe,* (N.Y., 1975), pp. 117, 118 & 122.
54. Ibid., p. 126.
55. Ibid., p. 127
56. Ibid., p. 131.
57. Ibid., p. 141.
58. Ibid., p. 145.
59. Rev. J.B. Salpointe, *Soldiers of the Cross,* p. 197.
60. Ibid., p. 196.
61. Paul Horgan, *Lamy of Santa Fe,* (N.Y., 1975), p. 148.
62. Lamy letter to Purcell of February 1, 1852, (Notre Dame).
63. Paul Horgan, *Lamy of Santa Fe,* (N.Y., 1975), p. 148.
64. Lamy letter to Purcell of February 1, 1852 (Notre Dame).
65. Paul Horgan, *Lamy of Santa Fe,* (N.Y., 1975), p. 150.
66. Henry R. Wagner, *New Mexico Spanish Press,* (New Mexico Historical Review, 12, 1937), pp. 1-40.
67. Paul Horgan, *Lamy of Santa Fe,* (N.Y., 1975), p. 175.
68. Ibid., p. 172.
69. Ibid., p. 177.
70. Ibid.
71. Ibid.
72. Ibid.
73. Ibid., p. 178.
74. Ibid.
75. Ibid., p. 191.
76. Ibid., p. 178.
77. Ibid.
78. Ibid., p. 179.
79. Ibid.
80. Ibid., p. 180.
81. Ibid.
82. Ibid., p. 183.
83. Ibid.
84. Ibid., p. 184.
85. Ibid.
86. Ibid., p. 188.

87. Ibid., p. 194.
88. Ibid., p. 190.
89. Ibid., p. 196.
90. Ibid., p. 204.
91. Pedro Sanchez, *Memorias Sobre la Vida del Presbitero, Don Antonio Jose Martinez*, p. 20.
92. George Wilkins Kendall, *Narrative of the Texan-Santa Fe Expedition*, 1841, I, pp. 339-401.
93. Jose E. Espinosa, *Saints in the Valleys*, p. 32.
94. Paul Horgan, *Lamy of Santa Fe*, (N.Y., 1975), p. 212.
95. Ibid., p. 213.
96. Ibid.
97. Ibid., pp. 213-214.
98. Ibid., p. 169.
99. Ibid., pp. 222-223.
100. W.W.H. Davis, *El Gringo: or New Mexico and Her People*, pp. 58-59.
101. Ibid., p. 95.
102. Ibid., p. 58.
103. Paul Horgan, *Lamy of Santa Fe*, (N.Y., 1975), p. 220.
104. Ibid., p. 221.
105. Ibid., p. 222.
106. Ibid., p. 223.
107. Ibid.
108. Ibid., p. 224.
109. Ibid.
110. Delete
111. Paul Horgan, *Lamy of Santa Fe*, (N.Y., 1975), p. 224.
112. Ibid., pp. 227-228.
113. Ibid., p. 227
114. Copy of *Gazette* in A.A.S.F.
115. Lamy letter to Martinez of May 5, 1856, (A.A.S.F.).
116. Paul Horgan, *Lamy of Santa Fe*, (N.Y., 1975), p. 228.
117. Ibid.
118. Ibid., p. 229.
119. Ibid., p. 183.
120. Ibid., p. 89.
121. Ibid., p. 229.
122. Ibid., p. 232.
123. Ibid., p. 233.
124. Ibid., pp. 233-234.
125. Ibid., p. 235.
126. Ibid., p. 241.
127. Martinez letter to Lamy of October 1, 1856, (A.A.S.F.).
128. E.Boyd, *Popular Arts of Spanish New Mexico*, (Museum of New Mexico Press, 1974) p. 396.
129. The Servite Fathers, *Seminario de Nuestra Senora de Guadalupe*, Belen, New Mexico, (Ward Anderson Printing Co., 1930), p. 19.
130. Ibid.
131. Ibid.
132. Paul Horgan, *Lamy of Santa Fe*, (N.Y., 1975) p. 247.
133. Ibid., p. 241.
134. Martinez letter to Lamy of April 13, 1857, (A.A.S.F.)
135. Ibid.
136. Martinez letter to Machebeuf of May 2, 1857, (A.A.S.F.).
137. Ibid.
138. Ibid.
139. Martinez letter to Lamy of June, 1857, (A.A.S.F.).

140. Paul Horgan, *Lamy of Santa Fe,* (N.Y., 1975), p. 244.
141. Martinez letter to Lamy of April 13, 1857, (A.A.S.F.).
142. Paul Horgan, *Lamy of Santa Fe.,* (N.Y., 1975), p. 245.
143. Martinez letter to Ortiz of November 10, 1857, (A.A.S.F.).
144. Martinez letter to Lamy of March 29, 1858, (A.A.S.F.).
145. Paul Horgan, *Lamy of Santa Fe,* (N.Y., 1975), p. 260.
146. Ibid.
147. Ibid., p. 261.
148. Warren A. Beck, *New Mexico-A History of Four Centuries,* pp. 216-217.
149. Paul Horgan, *Lamy of Santa Fe,* (N.Y., 1975) p. 151.
150. Lamy letter to Purcell of April 10, 1853, (Notre Dame).
151. Ibid.
152. Paul Horgan, *Lamy of Santa Fe,* (N.Y., 1975), p. 262.
153. Ibid., p. 274.
154. Ibid., p. 276.
155. Ibid., p. 274.
156. Ibid., p. 276.
157. Martinez letter to Lamy of September 24, 1859, (A.A.S.F.).
158. Paul Horgan, *Lamy of Santa Fe,* (N.Y., 1975), p. 277.
159. Ibid., p. 285.
160. Ibid., p. 297.
161. Ibid., p. 407.
162. Book of Wis., chap. 2, ver. 10.
163. St. Luke, chap. 10, ver. 3.
164. St. Matthew, chap. 5, ver. 44.
165. Pedro Sanchez, *Memorias Sobre la Vida del Presbitero, Don Antonio Jose Martinez.*
166. Lorenzo de Cordova, *Echoes of the Flute,* p. 17.
167. Pedro Sanchez, Obituary and Eulogy of Padre Martinez.
168. Paul Horgan, *Lamy of Santa Fe,* (N.Y., 1975), pp. 430-431.
169. Dora Ortiz Vasquez, *Enchanted Temples of Taos.*
170. E.K. Francis, *Padre Martinez: A New Mexican Myth,* (New Mexico Historical Review, Vol. XXXI, October 1956).
171. Harvey Fergusson, *Rio Grande,* p. 221.
172. Quoted by Walker, Archbishop Lamy, p. 67.
173. From an interview with Mrs. Dora Martinez de Armijo, grandniece of Padre Martinez.
174. Weigle, Marta, *Los Hermanos Penitentes: Historical and Ritual Aspects of Folk Religion in Northern New Mexico and Southern Colorado,* Unpublished dissertation.
175. E. Boyd, *Popular Arts of Spanish New Mexico,* (Museum of New Mexico Press, 1974), p. 397.
176. Blanche C. Grant, *When Old Trails were New—The Story of Taos,* p. 114.

Book Titles Which Contain References to Padre Antonio Jose Martinez and Bishop Jean Baptiste Lamy

A. Padre Antonio Jose Martinez

Ahlborn, Richard E.
THE PENITENTE MORADAS OF ABIQUIU, Contributions from the Museum of History and Technology, Paper 63, Smithsonian Institute Press, Washington, D.C., 1968.

Anderson, Arthur J.O.
TAOS UPRISING LEGENDS, El Palacio, December 1946.

Antony, Father Claudius
KIT CARSON, CATHOLIC - New Mexico Historic Review, No. 4 - October 1935, University of New Mexico.

Bancroft, Hubert H.
HISTORY OF THE PACIFIC STATES, The History Co., Pub., San Francisco, 1888.

Barker, Ruth Laughlin
CABALLEROS, D. Appleton & Co., New York, 1931.

Beck, Warren A.
NEW MEXICO—A HISTORY OF FOUR CENTURIES, University of Oklahoma Press: Norman, 1962.

Bernard, Jacqueline
VOICES FROM THE SOUTHWEST, Scholastic Book Services, New York, 1972.

Bloom, Lansing Bartlett
FIRST PRESS—EDITORIAL NOTES, PP. 107-110, New Mexico Historical Review, Vol. XII, January 1937.

Bloom, Lansing Bartlett
NEW MEXICO UNDER MEXICAN ADMINISTRATION, 1821-1846, Old Santa Fe; a magazine of History, Archaeology, Genealogy and Biography. Editor, Ralph Emerson Twitchell, Volume I, 1913-1914. Volume II, 1914-1915, Old Santa Fe Press, Santa Fe.

Boyd, E.
THE FIRST NEW MEXICO IMPRINT, Princeton Library Chronicle 33 (1971): 30-40.
POPULAR ARTS OF SPANISH NEW MEXICO, Museum of New Mexico Press, Santa Fe, 1974.

Burton, E. Bennett
THE TAOS REBELLION, Old Santa Fe, Volume 1, 1913, pp. 176-209.

Chavez, Fray Angelico O.F.M.
ARCHDIOCESE OF SANTA FE, 1678-1900, Academy of Franciscan History, Washington, D.C., 1957, (An index to the archives of the Archdiocese of Santa Fe.)
MY PENITENTE LAND: REFLECTIONS ON SPANISH NEW MEXICO, Albuquerque University of New Mexico Press, 1974.
THE PENITENTES OF NEW MEXICO, New Mexico Historical Review, Vol. 29/21, April 1954.

Cordova, Gilberto Benito
ABIQUIU AND DON CACAHUATE: A FOLK HISTORY OF A NEW MEXICAN VILLAGE San Marcos Press, Cerrilos, New Mexico, 1973.

de Cordova, Lorenzo
ECHOES OF THE FLUTE, Ancient City Press, Santa Fe, New Mexico, 1972.

De Fouri, Rev. J.H.
HISTORICAL SKETCH OF THE CATHOLIC CHURCH IN NEW MEXICO, San Francisco, 1887.

Duell, Daniel Long
PINON COUNTRY, Sloan and Pearce, New York, 1941.

Espinosa, Gilberto
THE CURATE OF TAOS: THE STORY OF THE LIFE OF PADRE ANTONIO JOSE MARTINEZ AND OF HIS TIMES, Undated ms. at University of New Mexico.

El Faro, Trinidad, Colorado., Feb. 25, 1938 issue. Editorial by Luis Martinez (researcher on Padre Martinez).
COMIENZA DE NUEVO LA FUNCION (dealing with the organizational development of la Fraternidad Piadosa de Nuestro Padre Jesus Nazareno).

Fergusson, Erna
NEW MEXICO. A PAGEANT OF THREE PEOPLES, Alfred A. Knoph, New York, 1951.

Furgusson, Harvey
RIO GRANDE, Alfred A. Knoph, New York, 1933.

Fernandez, Augustin, Vicar General
REPORT OF PASTORAL VISITATION OF THE MISSIONS OF NEW MEXICO, 1826. Document quoted in Salpointe, p. 159.

Forrest, Earle R.
MISSIONS AND PUEBLOS OF THE OLD SOUTHWEST, Rio Grande press, Chicago, Illinois, 1962.

Francis, E.K.
PADRE MARTINEZ: A NEW MEXICAN MYTH, New Mexico Historical Review, October, 1956.

Gilbert , Fabiola Cabeza de Baca
NEW MEXICO CIVILIZATION, Santa Fe Scene, May 3, 1958, p. 12.

El Historiador (anonymous)
HISTORIA CONSISA DEL CURA DE TAOS, ANTONIO JOSE MARTINEZ, Taos, May 4, 1861.

Horgan, Paul
THE CENTURIES OF SANTA FE, E.P. Dutton & Co., Inc., New York, 1956.
LAMY OF SANTA FE: HIS LIFE AND TIMES, Farrar, Straus and Giroux, New York, 1975.

Hughes, Delbert Littrell
GIVE ME ROOM, The Hughes Publishing Co., El Paso, 1971.

James, George Wharton
NEW MEXICO—THE LAND OF THE DELIGHT MAKERS, The Page Co., Boston, 1920.

Jenkins, Myra Ellen and Schroeder, Albert H.
A BRIEF HISTORY OF NEW MEXICO, Univeristy of New Mexico Press, 1974.

Keleher, William A.
TURMOIL IN NEW MEXICO, 1846-1868, The Rydal Press, Santa Fe, New Mexico, 1952.

LaFarge, Oliver
SANTA FE—THE AUTOBIOGRAPHY OF A SOUTHWESTERN TOWN, Norman: University of Oklahoma Press, 1959.

Larson, Robert W.
NEW MEXICO'S QUEST FOR STATEHOOD, 1846-1912, University of New Mexico Press, Albuquerque, New Mexico, 1968.

Lavender, David
BENT'S FORT, Doubleday & Co., Inc., Garden City, New York, 1954.

Loyola, Sister Mary
THE AMERICAN OCCUPATION OF NEW MEXICO, II, New Mexico Historical Review, XIV, pp. 143-200.

Martinez, L. Pascual
REV. ANTONIO JOSE MARTINEZ, Lulac News 5; 3-6, September 1938.

Martinez, Luis
PADRE MARTINEZ OF TAOS, a manuscript in the WPA file, S-240 folkways.

Martinez, Severino
THE LAST WILL & TESTAMENT OF SEVERINO MARTINEZ, Translated and annotated by Ward Alan Minge in New Mexico Quarterly, Volume 33/1, 1963. (Detailed account of execution of will by the eldest son, Padre Antonio Jose Martinez.

McMurtrie, Douglas C.
THE HISTORY OF EARLY PRINTING IN NEW MEXICO, New Mexico Historical Review, Oct. 1929.

Moorhead, Max L.
NEW MEXICO'S ROYAL ROAD, TRADE AND TRAVEL ON THE CHIHUAHUA TRAIL, University of Oklahoma Press, Norman, 1958.

Perrigo, Lynn I.
TEXAS AND OUR SPANISH SOUTHWEST, Banks, Upshaw & Co., Dallas, Texas, 1960.

Prince, Bradford L.
NEW MEXICO'S STRUGGLE FOR STATEHOOD, Santa Fe, 1910
SPANISH MISSION CHURCHES OF NEW MEXICO, Torch Press, Iowa, 1915.

Publication of the Servite Fathers.
SEMINARIO DE NUESTRA SENORA DE GUADALUPE, Belen, New Mexico, Ward Anderson Printing Co., 1930. (Historical notes on Belen and environs).

Read, Benjamin
GUERRA MEXICO-AMERICANA, Santa Fe, 1910.

Reeve, Frank D. (editor)
THE CHARLES BENT PAPERS, New Mexico Historical Review, Vols. XXXI and XXXII, 1956-1957.

Romero, Cecil V., (editor)
APOLOGIA OF PRESBYTER ANTONIO J. MARTINEZ, New Mexico Historical Review, Vol. III, pp. 325-46, 1928.

Salaz, Ruben Dario
COSMIC—THE LA RAZA SKETCH BOOK, Blue Feather Press, Santa Fe, New Mexico, 1975.

Salpointe, J.B.
SOLDIERS OF THE CROSS: NOTES ON THE ECCLESIASTICAL HISTORY OF NEW MEXICO, ARIZONA AND COLORADO, 1898.

Sanchez, Pedro
MEMORIAS SOBRE LA VIDA DEL PRESBITERO, DON ANTONIO JOSE MARTINEZ, translated and annotated by Ray John de Aragon, The Lightning Tree, Santa Fe, New Mexico, 1978.

Steele, Thomas J. S.J.
SANTOS AND SAINTS, Calvin Horn Publisher, Inc., Albuquerque, 1974.

Swadesh, Frances Leon
LOS PRIMEROS POBLADORES—HISPANIC AMERICANS OF THE UTE FRONTIER, University of Notre Dame, Indiana, 1974.

Twitchell, Ralph E.
LEADING FACTS OF NEW MEXICAN HISTORY; OLD SANTA FE, New Mexican Archives, History of the military occupation of New Mexico.
OLD SANTA FE, Vol. II, 1914-1915, Old Santa Fe Press, Santa Fe, New Mexico.

Valdez, Santiago
LA VIDA DEL PRESBITERO ANTONIO JOSE MARTINEZ, February, 1878. Hunt. Lib., Ritch Collection, No. 262.

Vasquez, Dora Ortiz
ENCHANTED TEMPLES OF TAOS, MY STORY OF ROSARIO, The Rydal Press, Inc., Santa Fe, New Mexico, 1975.

Wagner, Henry R.
NEW MEXICO SPANISH PRESS, New Mexico Historical Review, Vol. XII, University of New Mexico, pp. 10-40, No. 1, January 1937.

Warner, Louis H.
ARCHBISHOP LAMY, pp. 69-88, Santa Fe New Mexican Publishing Corp., Santa Fe, New Mexico, 1936.

Weigle, Mary Marta
LOS HERMANOS PENITENTES: HISTORICAL AND RITUAL ASPECTS OF FOLK RELIGION IN NORTHERN NEW MEXICO AND SOUTHERN COLORADO, Unpublished doctoral dissertation, University of Pennsylvania, 1971.

B. Bishop Jean Baptiste Lamy

Bancroft, Hubert H.
HISTORY OF THE PACIFIC STATES, History Co. Publ., San Francisco, 1888.

Beck, Warren A.
NEW MEXICO—A HISTORY OF FOUR CENTURIES, University of Oklahoma, 1962.

Bloom and Donnelly
NEW MEXICO HISTORY AND CIVICS, U.N.M., 1933.

Boyd, E.
POPULAR ARTS OF SPANISH NEW MEXICO, Santa Fe, New Mexico, 1974.

Charles, Sister Peter Damian
DEATH COMES FOR THE ARCHBISHOP, A NOVEL OF LOVE AND DEATH, New Mexico Quarterly, Winter, 1966-67.

Chavez, Fray Angelico
ARCHIVES OF THE ARCHDIOCESE OF SANTA FE, 1678-1900.

Chavez and Adams
THE MISSIONS OF NEW MEXICO, 1776, U.N.M., 1956.

Chavez, Fray Angelico
THE SANTA FE CATHEDRAL, 1947.
SANTA FE CHURCH AND CONVENT SITES IN THE SEVENTEENTH CENTURIES, New Mexico Historical Review Vol. 24, April 1949.
THE UNIQUE TOMB OF FATHERS ZARATE AND DE LA LLANA IN SANTA FE, New Mexico Historical Review, Vol. 50, April 1965.

Cincinatti Archdiocesan Archives
LETTERS OF J.B. LAMY; LETTERS OF ANTONIO JOSE MARTINEZ TO BISHOP LAMY, 1853-1861; and TRACTS, CIRCULARS, NEWSPAPERS ARTICLES IN OPPOSITION OF THE LAMY ADMINISTRATION, 1857-1860; LETTERS OF BISHOP PURCELL, University of Notre Dame Archives.

Defouri, V. Rev. James H.
HISTORICAL SKETCH OF THE CATHOLIC CHURCH IN NEW MEXICO, San Francisco, 1887.

Dickey, Roland F.
NEW MEXICO VILLAGE ARTS, U.N.M., 1949.

El Palacio
NEW NOTES ON BISHOP LAMY'S FIRST YEARS IN NEW MEXICO, Vol. 65 February & March 1958, pp. 26-33, 73, 75.

Fergusson, Erna
NEW MEXICO—A PAGEANT OF THREE PEOPLES, New York, Alfred A. Knoph, 1966.

Fergusson, Harvey
RIO GRANDE, New York, William Morrow & Co., 1955.

Fierman, Floyd S.
THE TRIANGLE AND THE TETRAGRAMMALON, New Mexico Historical Review, Vol. 37, 1962.

Forrest, Earle R.
MISSIONS & PUEBLOS OF THE SOUTHWEST, Ohio, 1929.
MISSIONS & PUEBLOS OF THE SOUTHWEST, Rio Grande Press, 1962.

Fulton and Horgan
NEW MEXICO'S OWN CHRONICLE

Grant, Blanche C.
WHEN OLD TRAILS WERE NEW—THE STORY OF TAOS, New York, 1934.

Hammond and Donnelly
THE STORY OF NEW MEXICO—ITS HISTORY AND GOVERNMENT, UNM, 1936.

Hewett, Edgar L. and Fisher, Reginald G.
MISSION MONUMENTS OF NEW MEXICO, UNM, 1943.

Horgan, Paul
THE CENTURIES OF SANTA FE
LAMY OF SANTA FE, HIS LIFE AND TIMES, N.Y., Farrar Straus and Giroux, 1975.

Horn, Calvin
NEW MEXICO'S TROUBLED YEARS, Albuquerque, Horn & Wallace, 1963.

Howlett, Rev. W.J.
LIFE OF THE RIGHT REV. JOSEPH P. MACHEBEUF, O.D., 1908.

Keleher, Julia
BACKGROUND FOR A BEST SELLER, New Mexico Magazine, March 1955.

Keleher, William A.
THE FABULOUS FRONTIER, Rydal Press, Santa Fe, 1945.
TURMOIL IN NEW MEXICO, 1846-1868, Santa Fe, 1952.

Kubler, George
THE RELIGIOUS ARCHITECTURE IN NEW MEXICO, UNM Press, 1972.

La Farge, Oliver
SANTA FE—THE AUTOBIOGRAPHY OF A SOUTHWESTERN TOWN, University of Oklahoma, 1959.

Lavash, Donald R.
A JOURNEY THROUGH NEW MEXICO HISTORY, Portales, New Mexico, Bishop Publ. Co., 1971.

Martinez, Antonio Jose
LETTERS (1856-58) BROADSIDES (in Gaceta de Santa Fe); **TRACTS** (Taos, 1859-61). All in reproduction of manuscripts or typed copies. Santa Fe Archdiocesan in New Mexico.

New Mexico Magazine
THE BISHOP'S CHAPEL, January 1964.

New Mexico State Records and Archives
Santa Fe Archdiocesan Archives

Owens, Sister Lilliana
JESUIT BEGINNINGS IN NEW MEXICO, 1867-1882, El Paso, Texas, Revista Catolica Press, 1950
OUR LADY OF LIGHT ACADEMY, Santa Fe, New Mexico, Historical Review, Vol. XIII, April 1938.

Pacific States Publishing
HISTORY OF NEW MEXICO—ITS RESOURCES AND PEOPLE, 1907

Perrigo, Lynn D.
OUR SPANISH SOUTHWEST, Banks, Upshaw & Co., Dallas, 1960

Prince, L. Bradford
SPANISH MISSION CHURCHES OF NEW MEXICO, Torch Press, Iowa, 1915.

Read, Benjamin
ILLUSTRATED HISTORY OF NEW MEXICO, Santa Fe, 1912.

Ritch, William G.
DISPATCH TO THE NEW YORK HERALD, June 21, 1875, Ms. Huntington Library, San Marino, California.

Ryan, Rev. Paul E.
HISTORY OF THE DIOCESE OF COVINGTON, KENTUCKY, Covington, 1954.

Salpointe, Most Rev. J.B. D.D.
SOLDIERS OF THE CROSS

Segale, Sister Blandina
AT THE END OF THE SANTA FE TRAIL, Columbus, Ohio, Columbian Press, 1932.

Col. Sena Cataloguing documents.
LETTER BY DON JUAN FELIPE ORTIZ, Vicar General at Santa Fe to parish priests, 1851, Archives of the Archdiocesen.

Swadesh, Frances Leon
LOS PRIMEROS POBLADORES, U. Notre Dame Press, Indiana, 1974.

Warner, Louis Henry
ARCHBISHOP LAMY; AN EPOCH MAKER, Santa Fe, Santa Fe New Mexican Pub. Corp., 1936.

Weigle, Marta
BROTHERS OF LIGHT—BROTHER OF BLOOD, THE PENITENTES OF THE SOUTHWEST, UNM Press, 1976.

Supplementary Sources

Alaman, Lucas
DISERTACIONES SOBRE LA HISTORIA DE LA REPUBLICA MEXICANA.
Mexico, 1844. Historia de Mexico, desde los primeros movimientos que prepararon su independencia en el ano 1808, hasta la epoca presente. Mexico, 1849.

Allison, W.H.H.
SANTA FE AS IT APPEARED DURING THE WINTER OF THE YEARS 1837 and 1838, as narrated by the Late Colonel Francisco Perea in Old Santa Fe, 11, Oct. 1914.

Anderson, G.B.
HISTORY OF NEW MEXICO, Pacific States Co., Los Angeles, 1907.
ARCHIVES OF THE ARCHDIOCESE OF SANTA FE. L.D.-(1712,1), (1758, 3), (1821, 29), (1827, 7, 10); L.D.D.-(Post 1851), (1852), (1853, 17). Accounts-(Book XXV, Box 2, Santa Cruz, 1768-1831), (Book LXII, Box 5, "Acts of the Guevara Visitation of New Mexico, 1817-20."), (Book LXIV, Box 5, "Acts of the Fernadez de San Vicente Visitation, Cont.)

Barreiro, Antonio
OJEADA SOBRE NUEVO MEXICO, 1832 in three New Mexico Chronicles, translated and edited by H. Bailey Carroll and J. Villasena Huggard, Quivira Society, Albuq., 1942.

Blacker, Irwin R.
THE BOLD CONQUISTADORES, Bobbs-Merrill, 1961.

Boyd, E.
THE NEW MEXICO SANTERO, Museum of New Mexico Press, 1969.

Calderon de la Barca, Fanny
LIFE IN MEXICO, Doubleday, New York, 1966.

Castor, Henry
THE FIRST BOOK OF THE SPANISH-AMERICAN WEST, Franklin Watts, 1963.

Clark, Ann
THESE WERE THE VALIANT, Calvin Horn, 1969.

Court Records
Santa Fe, Taos, New Mexico, Historical Society Library.

Crandall, Elizabeth
SANTA FE, Rand McNally, 1965.

Cuevas, P. Marino S.J.
HISTORIA DE LA IGLESIA EN MEXICO, El Paso, Texas: Editorial "Revista Catolica", 1928, 5 vols.

Davis, W.W.H.
EL GRINGO: OR, NEW MEXICO AND HER PEOPLE, Rio Grande, 1963.

DISCIPLINARY DECREES OF THE GENERAL COUNCILS
St. Louis: Herder, 1937.

Ellis, Florence Hawley
SANTEROS OF TOME, in the New Mexico Quarterly, V. XXIV/3, 1954.

Espinosa, Aurelio M.
LOS HERMANOS PENITENTES, Catholic Encyclopedia, Vol. XI, p. 635.

Espinosa, Jose E.
SAINTS IN THE VALLEY, University of New Mexico Press, 1960.

Federal Writer's Program, W.P.A.
NEW MEXICO STATE GUIDE, Hastings House, 1940. Grant, Blanche, Taos Today, Taos, 1925.

Flinn, D.J.
  PENITENTES IN TAOS, Harper's Weekly, about 1896.

Gregg, Josiah
  COMMERCE OF THE PRAIRIES, 1840. Vol. I, p. 47.

Henderson, Alice Corbin
  BROTHERS OF LIGHT, Rio Grande, 1963.

Jaramillo, Cleofas
  SHADOWS OF THE PAST, Santa Fe, 1941.

Kendall, George Wilkins
  NARRATIVE OF THE TEXAS-SANTA FE EXPEDITION, 1841, Harper's, New York, 1844.

Lucero-White, Aurora
  LOS HISPANOS, Sage Books, 1947.

Lummis, Charles F.
  LAND OF POCO TIEMPO, Scribner, 1925.
  THE SPANISH PIONEERS, Chicago: A.C. McClurg & Co., 1899.

Maas, Otto P.
  VIAGES DE MISIONEROS FRANCISCANOS A LA CONQUISTA DE NUEVO MEXICO, Sevilla, 1915.

Ocaranza, Fernando
  ESTABLECIMIENTOS FRANCISCANOS EN EL MISTERIOSO REINO DE NUEVO MEXICO, Mexico, 1934.

Otero-Warren, Nina
  OLD SPAIN IN OUR SOUTHWEST, Rio Grande, 1963.

Schroeder, Henry J.
  CANONS AND DECREES OF THE COUNCIL OF TRENT, St. Louis: Herder, 1941.

Thurston, Herbert, S.J.
  LENT AND HOLY WEEK, New York: Longmans, Green & Co., 1914.

THE VIGIL PAPERS
  New Mexico Historical Society Lib.

Printed in the United States
77993LV00007B/53